D0910408

The Practicing Poet

Also by Diane Lockward

The Uneaten Carrots of Atonement
Temptation by Water
What Feeds Us
Eve's Red Dress

Greatest Hits: 1997-2010 (Chapbook)
Against Perfection (Chapbook)

The Crafty Poet: A Portable Workshop
The Crafty Poet II: A Portable Workshop

The Practicing Poet

Writing Beyond the Basics

edited by

Diane Lockward

Terrapin Books

© 2018 by Diane Lockward
Printed in the United States of America
All rights reserved.
No part of this book may be reproduced in any manner,
except for brief quotations embodied in critical articles
or reviews.

Terrapin Books
4 Midvale Avenue
West Caldwell, NJ 07006

www.terrapinbooks.com

ISBN: 978-1-947896-07-9
LCCN: 2018947681

First Edition

Contents

IV. Working with Sentences and Line Breaks

V. Crafting Surprise

VII. Dealing with Feelings

VIII. Transforming Your Poems

X. Publishing Your Book

Introduction

Readers familiar with my previous craft books, *The Crafty Poet: A Portable Workshop* and *The Crafty Poet II: A Portable Workshop*, will recognize the ten-part organization of this new book, with each section devoted to a poetic concept. These section concepts begin with "Discovering New Material," "Finding the Best Words," and "Making Music." The concepts become progressively more sophisticated, moving on to "Working with Sentences and Line Breaks," "Crafting Surprise," and "Achieving Tone." The following sections include "Dealing with Feelings," "Transforming Your Poems," and "Rethinking and Revising."

The final section, "Publishing Your Book," assumes that readers are working towards a manuscript. April Ossmann, both a poet and a book editor, provides an excellent overview of the subject in her piece on manuscript organization. This section also includes my own contribution on book promotion and ends with a piece by Adele Kenny on how to give an effective reading, a skill you'll need once your book is published.

Each of the ten sections includes three craft tips, each contributed by an accomplished poet, such as Maggie Smith, Diane Seuss, Molly Peacock, Patrick Donnelly, and Campbell McGrath. Each of the thirty craft tips is followed by a model poem found in a book or journal. Collectively, these poems provide an anthology of contemporary poetry and reflect *The Practicing Poet*'s underlying philosophy that the craft of poetry can be taught and its best teacher is a good poem. Each model poem is followed by an analysis of its craft and then a prompt that asks the reader to practice the skills demonstrated in the model poem. Two sample poems follow each prompt. Contributed by subscribers to my monthly Poetry Newsletter, these sample poems illustrate some of the possibilities of the prompts and should provoke thought and discussion.

What comes next is a feature new to this book: a Top Tips list. I invited ten prominent poets to each contribute a list of their best pieces of poetry wisdom. They sent astonishing lists, beyond my already high expectations. You will want to revisit these lists often. Some of them are wide-ranging, e.g., Robert Wrigley's "Sixteen Tips, Quips, and Pontifications" and Patricia Smith's "Ten Things about Poetry." Other lists are more sharply focused, e.g., Oliver de la Paz's "Ten Shortcuts: A Busy Body's Guide to Writing Poetry," which focuses on time management for poets who lead busy lives, and Albert Rios's "Finding Your Book," which suggests a number of organizational options for your manuscript. There is nice variety in the presentation of these lists. Some are formatted as numbered lists while Dorianne Laux offers hers as a prose poem and Jan Beatty offers hers as an open form poem.

Each section ends with a Bonus Prompt. These are short writing activities which can be repeatedly recycled. They are useful for those days when you have no fresh ideas of your own. They leave you with no excuses for writer's block. They may also leave you with some keeper poems.

Like my two earlier books, this one is geared towards the practicing poet who already has a knowledge of the basic skills of poetry. This book pushes poets beyond the basics and encourages the continued reading, learning, and writing of poetry. Suitable as a textbook in the classroom or as a guidebook in a workshop, it should also be useful as an at-home tutorial for the practicing poet working independently. As the sections are arranged sequentially, the book may be covered in order from beginning to end; however, as each section also stands on its own, it's possible to work with the book in any order a user chooses.

The craft tips, poems, and top tips lists include the work of 113 contemporary poets. Three years in the making, this book would not exist without the generous contributions of so many poets. Whether you are using this book in a classroom or a workshop or at home, may it advance your work as a practicing poet.

Now turn the page and let the reading, learning, and writing begin.

Diane Lockward

I. Discovering New Material

The chief enemy of creativity is good sense.

—Pablo Picasso

Craft Tip #1: Word Banks: Smashing Words Together to Create a Spark

—Sandy Longhorn

From time to time, I've found myself in a lull, desperate to write new poems while fearing my well has been scooped dry. One surefire method of breaking that silence has never failed me: word banks.

There are many variations of this activity, but I first encountered it while teaching in the University of Arkansas' Writers in the Schools program as a graduate student working on my MFA. One day while visiting a middle-school classroom, my teaching partner wanted to talk about line breaks, so he made a word bank of seven words on the board and asked the students to write a seven-line poem where each of these words served as an end word. The words, all strong nouns and verbs, could be used in any order, and endings could be changed for number and tense. We gave the students seven minutes; under such a time constraint, the internal critic falls silent.

Free of poetic definitions and with an emphasis on play rather than seriousness, those students *got it*. They created unexpected line breaks, images, and metaphors that blew me away.

Moving forward from this basic use of a word bank, I often create a more elaborate exercise in my journal when I feel stymied. The focus on this larger collection of words is to mine them from various sources. For example, I pick a book of poetry, an essay from a literary magazine, and a more scientific or non-literary source. I then skim each source and pick out strong nouns and verbs that strike my tongue, with perhaps a spicy adjective thrown in here and there.

There are two methods for collecting these words. Both require writing by hand. The first method is to create columns of words. The second method depends on words jotted randomly across the page, as if they have spilled. At first, this requires conscious effort, especially if writing on ruled paper. However, after the initial handful of words is splayed there, the rest tend to fall where they may, with words from all my sources bumping against each other.

As I transcribe these mined words in my journal, either in columns or in a jumble, I keep half an eye out for random sparks, the kind of sparks that form when two words that wouldn't normally be found together smash against each other and suggest an image or metaphor that strikes me as fresh. When this happens, I circle the words and draw arrows or connecting lines to note the flash. I continue gathering words until the page is full to bursting, always on the lookout for energetic twists and turns and annotating those word-based firings as I go along.

I'm never happier than with a full page of scattered words in front of me. The possibilities! I flip to a blank page and begin word doodling based on my sets of random sparks. Often, there is a line already waiting for me as my mind has been processing the combinations all along. If such a line inspires a solid draft, so be it. If such a line inspires a few more lines and then the fire peters out, I simply flip back to the word bank in all its messy glory and see what I can find to add more kindling to the process.

Inevitably, while this exercise is based on randomness and chance, my own obsessions find their way through, and my own poetic voice is strengthened by the play rather than weakened. While every draft produced from a word bank might not make it to publication, this process has a strong track record of stimulating new poems.

Poem and Prompt

Pediatrics

You told me your pain was like
  an alligator, with sharp teeth

and beady eyes. He crawled up
  from the Everglades, moved

into your body. The doctors
  tried to catch him; the nurses,

to hold him down. Then your pain
  was like a bear who'd tear

a happy family to shreds
  over the honey ham in the cooler.

The bear had found a bees' nest,
  kept pawing it with his claws.

Your pain is not like an animal anymore.
  Your eyes burn amber

when you're able to lift your graphite lids.
  You're all swollen stomach,

an almost empty oxygen tank,
  a dark splinter in white sheets.

—Emari DiGiorgio

Is there anything harder for a parent to witness than a child's
pain? That's the topic DiGiorgio tackles in this poem. In addition,
she takes on the difficult second person point of view, addressing
the child as *you* as he lies in bed in the hospital. Although the

speaker remains unidentified and never enters the poem, we feel the presence of the mother. She serves as a filter, repeating to us what the child has said in his attempt to describe his pain.

Because the child does not have the vocabulary to concretely describe his pain, he does so in two similes, the first comparing the pain to that caused by an alligator's bite, the second to that caused by a bear's claws. Each simile is expanded with details.

When we get to stanza 7, the animal similes are dropped as the mother attempts to describe what she sees in that bed—her child's eyes burning *amber*, his *graphite lids*, his *swollen stomach*. The poem then ends with a powerful metaphor: the child is *a dark splinter in white sheets*.

Notice the format of the poem—two-line stanzas with each second line indented, all lines fairly even in length. This is perhaps the poet's attempt to impose control on what she cannot control.

✎ ✎ ✎

For your own poem, think of someone whose difficult situation you witnessed. This could be a child but doesn't have to be. The pain could be physical. Or it could be emotional, perhaps a loved one's fear, jealousy, anger, love, desire.

Use the second person point of view, addressing the person as *you*. See if you can establish both distance and closeness as DiGiorgio does.

Follow the pattern DiGiorgio establishes in her poem. Rely first on similes to express the discomfort of the situation. Create at least two and elaborate on each one. Then move to concrete details. End with a metaphor.

As you revise your poem, carefully arrange the words. You might borrow the same format or you might vary it. But keep the pattern tight for this poem.

Alternatively, you might want to imply lack of control by using a wild format.

Sample Poems

The Divorce

for Nora

Before, her pain was like quicksand,
ground dissolving beneath her feet.

It consumed her, swallowed her words
into bottomless cold. She sank slowly.

I cast her lifelines, but they slipped
through her hands. No matter how

she fought against the inertial weight
of elements, she could not haul herself out.

Then, she left him, and her pain was like
the shock the collar delivers the dog

when she runs through the electric fence—
quick and stunning, lung-emptying.

Now, her pain is not like that.
She speaks in short words—*sad, yes, no.*

Her black pickup truck yawls along
the canyon highway, into the desert.

Love and sorrow hold hands in the cab,
as if they belong together always.

—Kathy Nelson

Not Your Pain

for Phil

You are trying to climb
      out of the body that pain

has invaded like wildfire,
      licking your limbs, your

bones, searing your brain.
      Thrashed on the white-

sheeted bed, you curl to
      a ball tighter than fetal,

waiting on antidote, prick
      of the merciful needle

brought by the redheaded
      nurse who hasn't yet

gotten permission. *Not
fire*, you tell me, *it claws*

more like lightning
      striking a live pine,

stripping spirals of bark
      from its trunk. *Where*

is she?—crazy with burn,
      you're sure our nurse

is waylaid, too busy
      to banish your pain.

If only I knew
      how to peel pain away—

I kneel at your side,
       I lay hopeless hands

on your head, clenched
       flank, murmur this: *you*

are not your pain, this
       foot's free from pain,

this calf, there is none
       in your throat, your fist,

your shoulder, pain burns
       only here, at your belly's

stitched scars, a pain
       limited, local, you can

box it to burn in a cellar,
       make it a candle rowed

into a dark far from the
       body, not lodged in your

soul. All that I have,
       this handful of words.

—Judith Montgomery

Craft Tip #2: Know More

—Cynthia Marie Hoffman

We've all heard the old creative writing adage *write what you know*, and I agree with the basic tenet. It has to do with writing poems that are believable, authentic. But writing only what you already know limits the scope of your poem. So I'd like to make an amendment: *know more*.

My first two books of poetry were heavily informed by research. The first, *Sightseer*, tells the history of the places I'd visited on my travels. The second, *Paper Doll Fetus*, speaks from the world inside the womb and traces birth and midwifery back in time. Research was necessary for these two books because their very subjects required me to know more than my own story.

But you might be thinking research isn't right for you. After all, if you're not writing outright historical poems or poems based on science or medicine or architecture, aren't you sitting pretty, right in the *write-what-you-know* sweet spot?

We write (and read) in order to discover new things about ourselves and our world. As it turns out, we can always learn more about even the most seemingly mundane things that find their way into our poems.

Take, for example, a fly walking on a window pane. Ordinary as can be. I wanted to put such a fly into one of my poems for *Paper Doll Fetus*. The poem itself already depended on research. I was writing about abortion, and I needed to understand what that looked like. So I researched images of fetuses, many of which were placed beside quarters to show how small their bodies were. The crux of the poem, which came to be called "The Aborted Fetus Lays Its Tiny Hand upon the Cheek of George Washington," rose from looking at those photographs. Images came into the poem that I wouldn't have thought of on my own, like the powder in the former president's hair (I researched that, too), his face on the coin. But there is also this fly beating against a window, and the fly is important because its struggle is like that of the aborted human body, both of them shut out from life.

Like you, I've seen hundreds of flies in my lifetime, dozens of flies trying in vain to escape through a closed window. It would have been easy to think I already knew all I needed to know about flies in order to put one in a poem. And that was probably true. But if I hadn't taken a few moments to learn a bit about the mechanism by which a fly's feet cling to glass, I wouldn't have come up with the closure I needed in the ending lines: *The fly drags the delicate hairs of its feet / across the glass a trail of sweaty little footprints.* Insects have hairs and sticky pads on the bottoms of their feet! Before I learned that, I had never thought of a fly leaving footprints. Although the poem is primarily about the human body as evidence, I was now able to make this fly also leave its own bodily trace behind. This new knowledge helped me deepen the connection between the two main things happening in the poem.

So research, even in the smallest forms, can breathe new ideas into your poems. But those new ideas must make believable and authentic meaning. Be careful not to simply download interesting facts into your poems. Ask, how does this trivia tidbit help propel and intensify the argument or discovery of my poem? If it doesn't pass this test, it doesn't belong in your poem.

Now that I've sung the praises of research, a few more words of warning: First, it's easy to get overly obsessed with looking up information. It's exciting to immerse yourself completely in the experience of discovery through research. But the poems—and the experience of discovery inherent in the writing process itself—must come first. If you're more excited about your subject than the poems you're writing about that subject, it's time to reconsider. Also, research can be a great way to procrastinate, so watch how many hours you spend tumbling down the internet rabbit hole instead of writing. Successful research should bring you closer to your ideas, not distract you from them.

And finally, a word on diction. As poets, we love language. And it can be very tempting to get out the thesaurus, look up the etymology of words, become enamored with fascinating but little-known or ultimately cryptic scientific terms. *Petrichor! Occultation! Chatoyant!* When you find yourself getting caught up in the word itself, take a step back. Personally, I love big ideas expressed with simple words. To go back to the example of the fly on the window pane, *sweaty little footprints* is not the scientific term. But research is what got me there.

Research is simply a way of learning more about the world, of reaching outside yourself for something new. It doesn't have to be a daunting task; it can be as small as a gesture. First, know more. Then sneak your new knowledge into your poems in such a way that everyone believes you knew the information all along. Make it look easy. The best craft is invisible, and so is the best research. And there is a place for it in every day, possibly in every poem, sometimes where you'd least expect it.

Poem and Prompt

Apostrophe to S

I saw you first, S, in Genesis, at the end of
the heavens, before earth was written.
You doubled in darkness, witnessed
your form in the serpent. Now you return

each year, late in August, to start September,
then crawl inside burnt grass to sleep.
In the sound of rain you are rain's.
You were never mine but my name's.

I remember you nude, grafted to Sarah
in a shotgun apartment in Minnesota,
remember you white, inscribed in ice
after a skater crisscrossed the rink.

You bookend seasons, songs, seconds, belong to
the hiss. I met you twice in Saint Louis, once
at the casino turnstile as the bouncer's boss's
camera's lens distorted my face,

once in a rodent's pelvic bone in an owl pellet
in weeds at dusk. You descended from Sigma
descended from Phoenician descended from a
pictogram of a tooth. When I miss you

I press my teeth together. You clung to my brother
when he changed his name back to Stephan
from Steve. You're in sickness but never health,
worse but not better, neither have nor hold,

nor do you know you are sleep's, time's,
dread's, snow's, yes's, and no's equally.
Like any good act of possession, you ruin
what you love, then leave silently in debris.

—Ted Mathys

Consider the way Mathys plays with the concept of apostrophe in this poem. He uses it as both a figure of speech and a mark of punctuation. The entire poem is an apostrophe or direct address to the letter *s* and lots of words include an apostrophe.

The poem includes an abundance of words containing the letter *s*. There are words that begin with *s*, others that end with *s*, and some that contain an *s* in the middle. There are even words that begin and end with *s*: *You bookend seasons, songs, seconds.* And there are words that have two *s*'s in a row: *darkness, witnessed,* and *grass.*

The poet also doubles the double *s* sounds as in *crisscrossed* and *possession.* Finally, he uses many words that end with apostrophe *s* ('*s*): *rain's, name's,* and *rodent's.* This abundance of *s* sounds has a powerful auditory effect on the poem. Read it aloud and listen for the hissing consonance that runs throughout.

Mathys has a fondness for symmetry and several times gives us three items in a row. For example, we have *bouncer's, boss's, camera's* and *You're in sickness but never health, / worse but not better, neither have nor hold.* The poet doubles the number in the series and gives us *sleep's, time's, / dreads, snow's, yes's, and no's equally.*

Symmetry is also seen in the way Mathys formats the poem into 4-line stanzas, thus adding a formal touch to his play.

Finally, notice that in stanza 5 Mathys traces the lineage of the letter *s.*

For your alphabet poem, choose a single letter as your subject. Make a list of words that contain that letter. Put the words in a vertical list, one word per line. Then go through the list, spontaneously jotting down ideas next to as many words as you can, e.g., add an image suggested by the word, add a rhyme or near rhyme, add colors with that letter.

Research the history of your letter. Use Wikipedia or do a Google search. Take some notes.

Title your poem "Apostrophe to ?" Replace the ? with your letter.

Now begin your draft by starting at the top of your list of words and working your way down. Write quickly without stopping to critique yourself. Be sure to directly address your letter.

Go through what you've produced and enhance images and capitalize on sounds. Incorporate the notes you took on lineage.

Work in some lists of three items.

Be sure that you have an abundance of words that contain your letter, some words that begin and end with the letter, some words that contain the letter in the middle, and some that double the letter.

As you revise, you might want to create a different title, one that's less like the title of the model poem.

Sample Poems

Homage to T

You are a total tease, T. Your telltale doubles
tantalize and titillate. You lead in try, fall
behind in quit. In country dance you touch
and turn but in jitterbug you twist and twirl.

Birds in your world twitter and tweet,
but you are scarcely presidential. You are
first to try, first to tears, last to fight, last
to discouragement. You are most tempestuous,

tempted to talk by torture, hopelessly missing
from remorse. As *the alphabet's twentieth letter*,
you assert yourself seven times, proving
you are the most commonly used consonant

and the second most common letter. I hear
you stutter as you flutter before a platter
of peanut butter treats. So much of you there!
Too bad it stops with such finality at the waist.

Subtracting you from the alphabet, we would
have to sand instead of stand, walk on fees instead
of feet, and travel would become a rip.
We know introspection is in your dictionary,

that you're thrilled we're so dependent on you,
yet you always seem bereaved, for you're never
privileged in love. Don't worry. Without you
we'd be on a long road going nowhere.

—Patricia L. Goodman

H: A Personal History

Hail! And what ho! Oh eighth letter of the English alphabet!
Hitching post edging my homuncular life!
We first met at the finish of my birth—my first breath,
August twenty-fourth, under Virgo's horoscope sign.

Hello, hale and hearty well-wisher! You schooled
me on happiness, honor, and—ha! ha!—humor.
At bedtime's silent hour, shh! I heard you
whisper *hush, little baby*, my mother's lullaby.

When I turned three, you,
the hub of my constant *why*.
In my ninth hot-pink summer, you floated plushy
horses across the sky, no hint in cirrus, cumulus, nimbus.

I hunger and you satisfy
with honeydew, hoecakes and ham.
They say you have a half-life:
lighten chai with half-and-half,

warn when roughhewn ideas are
half-baked
or I go off
half-cocked.

Hallowed be thy name!
At the head of halo,
resounding in hallelujah hymn,
twice-blessed in hagiography.

Your hazy ancestry: Semitic consonant *heth,*
harsh fricative in the pharynx like a piece of challah?
No. The Hellene's *eta / heta* vowel, the wiser choice.

I'll hitchhike to any hearth and home you furnish,
Spanish hacienda or humble Borneo Gurkha hut.
But at death, usher me to my high heavenly abode
or go, by hand basket, into the bowels of hell!

—Linda Simone

Craft Tip #3: Writing the Dragon

—Jennifer Militello

When I think of poems I have loved, they are poems that have gone right to the quick. They know packed away interiors and travel like oxygen in the blood. I talk often about reading poems with instinct instead of intellect, as a way of allowing the concrete narrative situation to be subsumed, as a way of recognizing and recreating the experiential complexities of our lives.

But how do we write this poem?

With images, with metaphors. With incongruence, and trust.

And by being led.

I remember my teacher Charles Simic saying that you can want to take your poem to church, but if the poem wants to go to the dog track instead, you have to follow. The poem knows best. It has the nose of a hound. Let it lead you once it catches its own scent. The poem is, oddly, tracking itself. Unclip the leash. Run when it runs. Crash wildly through the undergrowth. Try to keep it in sight.

The poem is a machine, and, like all machines, it needs to be fueled. Feed your poems with your obsessions. Feed them energy. Feed them interesting words. I try to keep language readily available when I write, that strange array of words needed to make the meaning the poem envisions. I trust what Robert Bly calls *leaps*. I trust that the images are puzzling their way into their own world. But I also string them together with a current of urgency.

If poetry is a religion, here are a few things that might make up my creed:

I believe in freewrites. Take the pressure off, go all out, see what's inside that cobweb-infested mechanism of the brain when you turn it over and shake it out. Feel raw. Go down into the animal of yourself. This is the best way to follow the writing and discover where it wants to go. Obsessions sometimes sleep deep in the cerebral cortex. Writing forward into who-knows-what pokes them with a stick and wakes them up. Sometimes you may feel you want to sneak around them as if they are the dragon sleeping atop the gold, so that you can leave with the treasure. But the real poem is the dragon itself.

I believe in lists. Lists build energy in that they take short breaths, repeatedly alight, are a bit like the minutes just before an airplane lands when you can feel the wheels make contact with the tarmac. Lists touch down. They build anticipation and take the brain in sudden directions, all while creating expectation for the next moment, and the next.

I believe in reference books. Facts, definitions, medical terms, geometric properties, labeled pictures of machine parts. All of these are reservoirs of language. And where there is language, there is metaphor. Naming is a replacement. All things represent something else.

I believe in odd pairings. I don't want my poems to be tidy or entertaining. I don't want them to go too easy on the brain. I believe the purpose of art is to disturb and to awaken. The more we place incongruent items side by side, the more we surprise. The more we surprise, the more we rethink. The more we rethink, the more we fully know. We see new sides when we hold an object up to the light. Angles are everything. Metaphor helps us turn over the stones we think we know.

Poem and Prompt

Variation on a Theme by Elizabeth Bishop

Start with loss. Lose everything. Then lose it all again.
Lose a good woman on a bad day. Find a better woman,
Then lose five friends chasing her. Learn to lose as if
Your life depended on it. Learn that your life depends on it.
Learn it like karate, like riding a bike. Learn to fall
Forever. Lose money, lose time, lose your natural mind.
Get left behind, then learn to leave others. Lose and
Lose again. Measure a father's coffin against a cousin's
Crashing T-cells. Kiss your sister through prison glass.
Know why your woman's not answering her phone.
Lose sleep. Lose religion. Lose your wallet in El Segundo.
Open your window. Listen: the last slow notes
Of a Donny Hathaway song. A child crying. Listen:
A drunk man is cussing out the moon. He sounds like
Your dead uncle, who, before he left, lost a leg
To sugar. Shame. Learn what's given can be taken;
What can be taken, will. This you can bet on without
Losing. Sure as nightfall and an empty bed. Lose
And lose again. Lose until it's second nature. Losing
Farther, losing faster. Lean out your open window, listen:
The child is laughing now. No, it's the drunk man again
In the street, losing his voice, suffering each invisible star.

—John Murillo

Murillo's title announces that his poem is based on one by Elizabeth Bishop. Thus, no attribution is necessary. We quickly recognize that the poem referred to is Bishop's well-known villanelle "One Art." Before we go further, please find and reread that poem.

Murillo not only keeps the theme of Bishop's poem but also repeats as she does the various forms of *to lose: loss, lose, lost, losing*. And he uses many words that begin with the letter *L: listen, learn, lean*. Like Bishop, he employs a catalog, imperatives given like directions, and colons (she uses one while he uses three). He even borrows an entire phrase: *Losing / Farther, losing faster*.

Notice, however, that while Murillo borrows theme, words, and techniques from Bishop, he abandons her villanelle form in favor of the one-stanza form.

✐ ✐ ✐

For your own theme variation poem, first choose a well-known poem, perhaps Frost's "Mending Wall" or "Stopping by Woods on a Snowy Evening," Dickinson's "Because I could not stop for Death," or Dylan Thomas's "Do not go gentle into that good night." Be sure to choose a poem that is sufficiently well-known that readers will be familiar with it.

Make a list of the techniques employed by your poet. As you draft your poem, borrow some of those techniques.

Let your theme be reminiscent of the theme of the original.

Borrow some words and phrases. Lift them right out. It's okay to do this as you've announced upfront what you're up to. Of course, don't overdo the borrowing.

Vary the form of the original in your new poem.

Use your title or perhaps an epigraph to announce the poet you're borrowing from.

Sample Poems

Disillusionment of 6:22 AM

after "Disillusionment of Ten O'Clock," by Wallace Stevens

The banisters are tragic like engines
that jump their rails. The curtains

a mangled blue Audi on the Blue Line
track. Of colors, I can say blue, can also

say green, say yellow, say black. What's
a landscape made of? DO NOT ENTER,

a parking strip, a wooden bench. None
of this was ever strange, except in his

mind; he never spoke of it, especially
not at work. Walked and walked,

a notebook in the pocket of his suit.
His wife was his muse, every periwinkle

for Elsie, their life an embroidered
credenza. Baboons strode in and out

of his dreams. Baboons and haunted
nightgowns. In his poems, blood

an abstraction, a concept, not
spurting out after the shrapnel.

Here and there, a tiger; here and there,
a drunk, a sailor asleep in his boots.

—Martha Silano
published in *Thrush*

Variation on a Theme by Dylan Thomas

Die fast. Die soon. Don't burn and rave.
Even light dies nightly every day. Now people,
Too, in movie theatres and concert halls, at
Parties, in churches, at restaurants eating
Nouvelle cuisine, in clinics, at school.
Die with your head attached to your body.
Lie down gently on carpet or linoleum, slate
Or asphalt. Quick now. Die before you're dealt
From the bottom of the deck. Rage drives a box
Truck and so all men should die easy, die early,
Whether cursed or blessed, untrapped by those
Who flare up briefly like a struck match.

—Sheila Kelly

Top Tips: How to Write a Poem in Nine Easy Lessons + One

—David Kirby

1. Acquire the mind of a poet. It's more important to have the mind of a poet than to write poems. Poets notice details. They make connections. They're on duty day and night.

Nothing is off-limits to a poet. Make a plan, but be open to accidents. Art is the deliberate transformed by the accidental.

2. Keep a bits journal. A bits journal is just that; it's a collection of random images, childhood memories, dreams, snatches of overheard conversations, quotes from books you've read or lectures you've heard, bathroom graffiti, mistranslations, thoughts that come out of left field, notes to yourself, and so on.

When your bits journal starts to get unwieldy, it's harvest time. Look for bits that speak to each other, maybe three or four that might coalesce into a poem.

3. Remember that all poems begin small.

Want to write a poem? Here's the formula: b + T = P

The *b* stands for *beginning* and is lower case because all beginnings are small. When he thought about the "Ode on a Grecian Urn," Keats didn't say, *I'm going to write about art and immortality*. He said, *I'm going to write about a vase*.

The *T* is for *time* and is upper case because any good poem requires lots of time.

And *P* is for *poem*. Or *good poem*, really: do you want to write anything less?

4. Complicate your poem. Freud says that dreams aren't determined but overdetermined, that is, that they don't have a single cause but many. That's why a typical dream will incorporate

a memory, an occurrence that happened just the day before the dream, the sudden appearance of someone you haven't heard from in years, a loud sound from just outside your bedroom, and so on.

A poem my college students love is "Understanding Al Green," by Adrian Matejka. It's a poem about an older boy telling a younger one how to get girls to like him.

Obviously my students like the fact that Matejka is addressing the perilous teen years that they've just left behind. But notice that he addresses that topic with everything at his disposal, including sex, romance, music, friendship, humor, violence (having scalding grits thrown on you can't be fun), maturity or its lack, and mainly, hope, because, more than anything else, the speaker expresses every kid's hope that he'll grow up cool and that, with the right music and a little luck, he'll talk somebody into loving him.

But Matejka's poem wouldn't say any of that unless it said all of it.

5. Tell stories. Jesus spoke in parables because when you speak in parables, it's the listener who comes up with the right answer, not the speaker.

Also, you need images if your poem is going to succeed, and stories supply those images automatically; you don't even have to think about it. Tom Petty said, *A good song should give you a lot of images. You should be able to make your own little movie in your head to a good song.* Same for poems.

6. Borrow. Our culture is an enormous warehouse of references: songs, movies, clichés, book titles, advertising jingles, jokes, memes, poems by those whom Keats called *the mighty dead*. Readers like it when you invoke a text or a cultural artifact they already know; it makes them feel smart. Then, when you suddenly pull your readers in an unexpected direction, they're delighted.

T. S. Eliot said, *Immature poets imitate; mature poets steal; bad poets deface what they take, and good poets make it into something better, or at least something different.*

Notice how much of this whole list draws from the words of others?

7. End powerfully. The last thing you want to do is have your poem simply stop.

James Wright's "Lying in a Hammock at William Duffy's Farm in Pine Island, Minnesota" ends, *I lean back, as the evening darkens and comes on. / A chicken hawk floats over, looking for home. / I have wasted my life.*

The last lines of Dorianne Laux's "Fast Gas" read, *an ordinary woman who could rise / in flame, all he would have to do / is come close and touch me.*

And Matthea Harvey ends "The Backyard Mermaid" this way: *She wants to get lost in that sad glowing square of blue. Don't you?*

A surprising reversal, the approach of a lover, a question: each of these three endings surprises and pleases the reader.

8. Write great stanzas. Your words are the content of your poem, your stanzas are that content's delivery system.

There are countless ways to format poems, from the solid block of the sonnet to the scattershot look of Charles Olsen and Marianne Moore. The idea is to make your poem look considered, not careless, because if readers get the idea that you don't care how your poem looks, then they won't care, either.

9. Show your work to someone else. All successful recording artists work with producers. The original version of one of Janis Joplin's biggest hits, "Piece of My Heart," ran longer than four minutes, which meant its radio play would be limited. Too, the chorus wasn't repeated often enough to become the irresistible hook in the version we know today.

Columbia Records executive Clive Davis put it to Joplin plainly: without a hit single, the album the song appeared on might sell two or three hundred thousand copies, whereas with a radio hit, it would do twice that, maybe more. Joplin wasn't pleased with the suggestion, but she went along. "Piece of My Heart" went to number twelve on the charts, and the *Cheap Thrills* album rose to number one, selling more than a million copies.

+1. If you follow these nine tips and keep at it, sooner or later, you'll be writing good poems. But why stop there? Don't you want to write a great poem?

Earlier I gave you the basic formula, $b + T = P$, or *beginning plus time equals poem*.

Now here's the advanced formula: $b + T^2 = P^2$.

In English, that means *beginning plus lots of time equals great poem*. The b doesn't change, though. Remember, all beginnings are small.

Bonus Prompt: The Junk Mail Poem

Don't let your junk mail go to waste. Let it pile up. Then on a day when you need some inspiration, grab a store catalog that's come in the mail. Go through it, making a list of words, phrases, and images that capture your attention.

Using what you've taken from the catalog, draft a poem, but don't let the poem be about the catalog. It might, instead, be about falling in love, ending a relationship, losing a friend, grieving for someone you cared about, moving to a new location, receiving bad news.

Such a poem might lend itself to a liberal use of metaphors and similes.

II. Finding the Best Words

Poetry is a deal of joy and pain, and wonder,
with a dash of the dictionary.

—Khalil Gibran

Craft Tip #4: Accruing the Right Words

—Lauren Camp

I generally write when I have something I am trying to cling to, either a situation that is very dear or one that is disturbing. Even at those times when the subject comes through so clearly, I don't have all the perfect words or the perspective I want.

On a daily basis, my schedule is overloaded and my brain jammed with thoughts and the details of various responsibilities. I read obsessively, as I have done since I was a child. And everywhere I go, I find little phrases that excite me. I think it would be accurate to say I scribble and gather more than I write. And that is, weirdly, just fine with me.

Right now, I am sitting at my desk. I am a neat person in general, but my desk is a collection of book piles and scraps of paper that hold brilliant possibilities. In front of me, I have fit onto a mini yellow post-it a sentence that seems ideal for a sonnet I recently drafted. On another scrap, I have scrawled four slant rhymes that I found in someone else's poem (*moon, hands, hen, suns*) as a reminder that there is tremendous music in such almost rhymes. That note reminds me to try this technique with a rhyme of my own, as a way to add a near chant into a poem. Another paper notes some images from a recent walk on the beach. I also wrote *pelting* because that is a wondrous term. I can't remember where I read it, but I feel certain it will enrich a poem soon. I chatter lines into my phone as I drive to the gym or the store, and I email those to myself, to work in somewhere.

Where do you get your language? It doesn't have to come fully formed out of your head onto your paper or your keyboard. You can accrue it. Keep a notebook or use the back of your grocery list or your palm for the crucial morsels. Look everywhere. Don't keep your mind from seeing what's available everywhere.

This all started when I began to revise ferociously, cutting captivating phrases that had no right being in the particular poem I was tackling. I couldn't bear to trash them, so I built a Word.doc repository of the slashed phrases, end to end, top to bottom. That document is now seventeen pages long and jammed with intriguing phrases that I sometimes further meld for other projects. This is my encyclopedia, the consummate, personal collection of language that sings for me. Though I don't own these words, I own their arrangement.

I love the rush when I slither elements from my Lines Encyclopedia or the scraps on my desk into a poem that needs some juice, some pizzazz, some improv elements. And when I'm ready to revise some more, I'll scan around me for another handful of possibilities that can lift the poem further than I ever could on first draft or with a careful, linear mind.

Am I embarrassed about my desk? Slightly, and also, no. How often do you get the chance to hoard a thing that makes your pulse rush? Something about this practice means I never stop writing even when it seems I am not writing but going to the doctor or working out or making dinner.

This method won't give me a subject, but it'll let me locate greater music and astonishing language and metaphor and image descriptors. Throughout this process, which I do intuitively, I will hold onto the poem's heart and meaning.

For me, it is the juxtaposition of so many possibilities that makes a poem luminous. If I were more organized in my approach, the poem might be flat. The reader might feel little when interacting with it. The phrases that randomly clutter my desk crowd into and energize a poem in progress and make the end result so much more than I ever thought feasible.

Try it. It's not often someone says, go ahead, be messy; store all that treasure. It's a worthwhile practice.

Poem and Prompt

Boketto

Outside my window it's never the same—
some mornings jasmine slaps the house, some mornings sorrow.

There is a word I overheard today, meaning lost
not on a career path or across a floating bridge:

Boketto—to stare out windows without purpose.
Don't laugh; it's been too long since we leaned

into the morning: bird friendly coffee and blueberry toast. A while
since I declared myself a prophet of lost cats—blind lover

of animal fur and feral appetites. Someone should tag
a word for the calm of a long marriage. Knowledge

the heat will hold, and our lights remain on—a second
sight that drives the particulars of a life: sea glass and salt,

cherry blossoms and persistent weeds. What assembles in the middle
distance beyond the mail truck; have I overlooked oceans,

ignored crows? I try to exist in the somehow, the might still be—
gaze upward to constellations of in-between.

—Susan Rich

The poet takes the odd word *boketto* and lets it stimulate her imagination and guide the poem. Commenting on her poem, Rich said, *The Japanese word,* Boketto, *describes something so familiar to me, it's as if a piece of myself has been returned. I've altered the definition by including that the gazing without purpose needs to happen by a window*. As the speaker gazes out the window, she records her thoughts.

One distinctive attribute of the poem is the use of compounds, e.g., *on a career path or across a floating bridge, bird friendly coffee and blueberry toast, sea glass and salt*.

The poet makes use of *chiasmus* which is defined as a rhetorical or literary figure in which words, grammatical constructions, or concepts are repeated in reverse order, in the same or a modified form. It is similar to antithesis. Note, for example, the first stanza's *some mornings jasmine slaps the house, some mornings sorrow*. Another interesting example occurs in stanza 5: *animal fur and feral appetites*. Note how the *a* and *f* of *animal fur* are reversed in *feral appetites*. This rhetorical device works well with the poet's use of compounds.

Is it surprising, then, that the poem is written in two-line stanzas?

Note the playful metaphors. For example, the speaker describes herself as a *prophet of lost cats* and a *blind lover of animal fur and feral appetites*.

Note also the use of punctuation—five dashes, three colons, and two semi-colons. The dashes add a touch of informality, while the colons and semi-colons sound a more formal note.

✎ ✎ ✎

For your own weird word poem, first choose a weird word to reflect on. Some choices might be *petrichor, virga, verdad, grok, borborygmus, mudita, verklempt, schadenfreude*, or *bonhomie*. Look up the meaning of your word. Add something to the definition, something of your own invention.

Now freewrite for 10-15 minutes.

From that unharnessed writing, extract your poem. As you draft, impose some order on the chaos of your freewriting.

Try to get in some compounds and some chiasmus.

Add a few playful metaphors.

Think about your punctuation. Don't stick to boring, predictable periods; make use of other options. Alternatively, you might dispense with punctuation.

Find a form that fits your poem.

Sample Poems

Here We Waited for Windsnap

Windthrow: toppled trunks, roots exposed,
like a patient lying on a spilled bedpan.
Windsnap, worse: folded bole or cracked
trunk, splinters puncturing pure space.

But late night breezes sounded amorous,
sleepers turning on satin,
and when I hoisted the racing spinnaker,
I felt blown free of debris.

That was before history started to hurt—
too many days at permanent wilting point;
my friend wrongly jailed as a suspect the night
his wife dove into the wind below the balcony edge.

Powerful gusts overpower boles, leeward roots
beyond driplines, sinker root severed.
One butterfly evolved away its wings,
so it would not be blown off Desolation Island.

Dad collapsed right after the flight; I slipped,
a hammock with just one tree. When a tree
snaps in a graveyard, does anyone call
to tell you about his broken stone?

Dying pines lose all their twigs, pare down,
and all Mom can do is flap her good hand.
I think she wants to applaud my flute song.
Slowly follow the taproot down, stretch
hard, hope for loose soil. See where first
color appears in the spark of the tiniest bud.

                        —Tina Kelley

Etui

Small hard box of clear plastic
with compartments for sewing needles
of different sizes for embroidery,

or hooks and eyes to pierce fabrics, to poke open
a pattern one might envision for others to see,
outline secured by buttons, bone bits, baby teeth,

gallstones. Storage for beads and findings, sorted by
color, size, glass or metal, waiting to be called.
Inlaid wooden chests and ceramic vaults

for storage, for secrets never spoken,
forbidden feelings, foreign coins, firkins filled
with the smallest pine cones, cockles collected.

Specialty coffins for stones, crystals, casks
for arcane knowledge of their powers. Comfort
in their snapping, securely shut.

—Joan Mazza

Craft Tip #5: Choosing Your Words

—Barbara Hamby

A poet's voice is made up of many choices. What is your subject—family, your experiences in Iraq, music? Is your line long and narrative or short and imagistic? What kinds of images do you use? Are you fixated on the sea? Or maybe you find travel an inspiration. And syntax—are your sentences long and digressive or short and crisp? Are you a funny poet or one who is utterly serious? Are you a free verse poet or one who experiments with form? All of these choices work together to make up the voice in your poems. But one of the most elemental decisions is diction or word choice. What kind of language do you use in your poems?

English

When asked what *Lolita* was about, Vladimir Nabokov said, *My love affair with the English language*. What is it about English that is so thrilling? For one thing it is Whitmanian in its inclusiveness. We steal from everyone. No sooner is a revision of the Oxford English Dictionary finished, but another one begins. English has an enormous vocabulary. Every year there is an article about new words that have been coined. English is a young language. The first sentence in English was a rune found on a coin and dated in 400 A.C.E., but once St. Augustine came to the British Isles and taught the Anglo-Saxons to read and write, there was no stopping them. Then William the Conqueror invaded Britain in 1066, and the French of the Normans came too.

Anglo-Saxon and Latinate Language

For several hundred years England was a two-part society. There was the court and the nobility, who spoke French, and the Anglo-Saxons, who worked the land and spoke English. But over time this division broke down, and a kind of mongrel language developed. Most Anglo-Saxon words have disappeared. Today we use only about 500 Anglo-Saxon words. However, these words are the ones that we use the most—words like *wife, husband, woman, man*, and all our prepositions—*to, of, with, about*. And most of our curses are Anglo-Saxon. If a word ends with a *k,* chances are it is Anglo-Saxon in origin. The words for farming and menial tasks are Anglo-Saxon—*cow, oxen, miller, bread*. Words to describe the court and the judiciary are French in origin. When a poem sounds highfalutin', chances are the poet is using a Latinate vocabulary.

Mixing Dictions

So what does this mean for poets writing at the beginning of the twenty-first century? English gives you a lot possibilities. Hemingway wrote using a stripped down version of English that has been very influential on both poets and fiction writers. T. S. Eliot's diction was refined, but he was a twentieth-century poet. The first line of his "Love Song of J. Alfred Prufrock" is an example of a mixing of diction:

> Let us go then, you and I,
> when the evening is spread out against the sky
> like a patient etherized upon a table.

The first two lines are almost Victorian in their syntax and diction, but that third line changes everything. You are expecting an extension of the beautiful evening, but it's not beautiful. It's numb and lifeless. Today this image seems tame, but in its time it shook things up. Medical words like *etherized* had no place in poetry.

Simple versus Complex

There is no right or wrong way. Some poets prefer simple language, and make no mistake, a simple poem can convey depths of meaning. Take, for example, William Carlos Williams' "The Red Wheelbarrow" or Emily Dickinson's "Wild Nights":

> Wild nights, wild nights
> Were I with thee
> Wild nights would be
> Our Luxury.

No complicated language there, but the passion is explosive.

High and Low

Many poets like to mix high and low diction. I once characterized my own work as an opera with music by Donizetti with a libretto by Groucho Marx. Opera is considered *high art* and *Horse Feathers,* though sublime, is something that many people can enjoy. I don't really go for the term *low*. Maybe *popular* would be better. Why shouldn't I write an "Ode to Barbecue" or an "Ode to Hardware Stores?" That is my choice.

How to Amplify Your Diction

You may be satisfied with your diction, but if you want to amplify your word choice, how do you go about that? One way is to make lists of words. I love the vocabularies of different professions. To use the language of masons to describe the wall between two people would be a way to begin to make your diction more complex.

I also love words in other languages that we don't even come close to in English. For example, I just used the Swedish word *magata* in a poem. It is the trail moonlight makes in water. We can say it in English but it takes six words.

Perhaps the thing that really transformed my diction was the abecedarian poem. This is a kind of acrostic in which each line of a 26-line poem begins with a subsequent letter of the alphabet, beginning with *A* and ending with *Z*. In my first book I wrote an abecedarian, and I found myself out of my mind with happiness. I had so much fun. Then I decided to write a sequence of 26 poems, one for every letter of the alphabet. It was the hardest thing I'd ever written. English may have a huge vocabulary, but it doesn't have that many words that begin with *x* or *k* or *j*. I found that the necessities of the form took me to places that were surprising, and not just in terms of diction.

Try an abecedarian poem. Try a poem that mixes high and popular culture, and be sure to be aware of the mix of Anglo-Saxon and Latin in your word choice. I love to feel as if I'm still playing when I write, trying new things, discovering words. Carry a notebook everywhere. You never know when a great word will pop into your world.

Poem and Prompt

Maraschino

Means, *liqueur distilled from small, black*
mascara cherries. Means, *cherries preserved*
in that liqueur. Means, *this is going to hurt*.
Rainiers, Golds, plump Royal Annes
are soaked in brine, bleached like bloodstained clothes
in calcium chloride and reeking sulfur dioxide
until their brightness leaches out and skins
are plasticized to snap between the teeth.
They steep in great vats of sweet dye,
red as Valentines and deadly toads,
swirling cold in a slow centrifuge
of sickly red.
          And here's the handsome man
who calls you *sugar*, calls you other things
when the lights are out, shaking a chromed bullet
of bourbon, vermouth, bitters, shattered ice.
He strains it into a cone-shaped glass that holds
a single maraschino, poison-bright.
It drowns in amber, bumps against the glass.
Yes, he expects you to eat it, even as
it settles like an excised lump preserved
for biopsy. He expects you to put on lipstick,
take the cherry whole into your mouth,
and work your tongue until you've tied the stem
into an impossible knot. Take your time.
He'll watch you do it. He can wait all night,
even if it takes the whole damn jar.

—Juliana Gray

The poem begins with a multi-part definition and then proceeds
to a description of the process by which a maraschino cherry is

made. Much of this information comes from a very useful research source—Wikipedia. However, using some poetic techniques, Gray moves this first stanza beyond mere definition and description.

The poet inserts a startling simile to describe how the color is leached out of the original cherries: they are *bleached like bloodstained clothes*. Another technique, one embodied in the simile, is the use of contrast. The cherries have lovely names like *Rainiers, Golds, and plump Royal Annes*, and they are not only *plump* but also *sweet*. However, other diction choices suggest an undercurrent of danger. The maraschinos, in another simile, are *red as Valentines and deadly toads*. The first half of that description suggests romance; the second half suggests death.

The second half of the poem marks a turn. Gray indicates the turn by using a dropped line, a line which brings romance into the poem: *And here's the handsome man / who calls you sugar*. And yet the same undercurrent of danger seen in the first half of the poem also runs throughout this half. The man offers the woman a *bullet / of bourbon* and *shattered ice*. The single cherry in the drink is *poison-bright*. Then look at the final simile as the cherry settles in the glass *like an excised lump preserved / for biopsy*.

🖉 🖉 🖉

For your own poem, choose an unusual food item, one that requires a preparation process, e.g., a cocktail onion, Kalamata olive, calamari, piccalilli, hummus, salsa, caper, pickled pepper, caramel candy. Look up your item in a dictionary and in Wikipedia. You might also do a Google search. Take notes on the meaning of the word and the steps in the process.

Now begin your draft with a multi-part definition. Then move to a description of the preparation process.

Now bring in your turn. Indicate the turn with a dropped line as Gray does or with a stanza break. In the second half of your draft, switch to romance. Make your food item part of a romantic scene. Describe the scene and the item's role in it.

As you revise, pay attention to diction. Work in some contrasting language to suggest that the item and the scene are appealing but also have a dark underside, some danger or unpleasantness.

Create three similes for each half of your poem. Then choose the best one from each group of three. Insert that simile into the poem and make it an integral part of the poem. You may, of course, keep more than one simile.

Does the two-part division work for your poem? If not, feel free to experiment with other formats. Play and revise until you find the form that feels just right.

Sample Poems

Capers

Capparis spinosa, a spiny shrub
of flower buds, tiny buds, green buds
brine-packed—
pickled, salted, puckery,
vegetal, intense, a little floral,
depth as in taste, character as in statesman,
tenacious, a survivor of tiny crevices,
of intensely arid, lengthy drought,
flowering in the sacred western wall
in Jerusalem—
native there and still,
2000 years of rooting, of witness.
Use as a seasoning or garnish

and only harvest by hand, these tiny nubs,
before the breakout of flower—
with elegant violet filament,
with flagrant thorny stems
and perhaps for mindfulness in the holy land,
one might taste the brine of history.
Hold it gently on the tongue before digesting.

And here's my guy at the dinner table
and he's not crazy about those little nubs
slipping into mealtime and I am hoping
I can change his palette as I cook up
a succulent puttanesca but it fails to entice
and I implore him to succor the wild, the sacred,
the passion surrounding those little buds,
the aroma of holy rancor
ingested into the diet of the day.

—Carol Seitchik

Citrus aurantium

means Seville orange. Means a small thick-
rinded citrus fruit with dimpled pocked orange
skin. Means this zest will be bitter, sour as
lemon missing the rasp. Adored by Brits who
know to wash, dry, slash through its equator,
pierce out the dozens of pectin-rich seeds to
save to cinch like innards in a muslin bag with
the segment membranes dredged after ex-
traction of the juice, boil with peel julienned
by a sharp knife, simmer with water until
strips lie translucent. Then add sugar and boil
all again, removing the seed pouch at last, to
fill scalded marmalade jars. In French the fruit
goes by *L'orange amère*, as if a bit like *amour*,
the petite glowing lanterns conspiring to craft
Grand Marnier, Triple Sec, and Cointreau.
But Andalusia's divine air and golden sun
succor the trees by the Guadalquivir River
where evenings are lovely for tapas in view
of flamenco dancers or historic structures
from rooftop bars.
            But here's the delicious
crime in the sweet bitterness, already at work
for days before toxicity shows: a flavonoid
in this orange, known as naringin, like a drain
on the battery, impairs the enzyme essential
for metabolizing your transplant medicine
cyclosporine, allowing its level inside you
to rise and poison your marrow's blood cell
production. But take your time, savor Seville
marmalade on toast tips, sip Grand Marnier
with your lover by the flicker of candlelight.
A dip in your counts may not kill you.

—Dianne Silvestri

Craft Tip #6: Using Etymology

—Natasha Sajé

Looking up every word you use and finding its history might give you the subject for a poem or a fresh turn when you are stuck. English is a very lexically rich language. Norse influence gave the English language basic words like *skin, egg,* and *knife.* Later, when the Norman French invaded England in 1066, French became the language of the court and the ruling class, and Germanic-based Old English was relegated to the so-called common people. For a period of 400 years, English both lost distinct letters and gained new spellings from the French. By Shakespeare's time, English had absorbed many Latin and Greek words by assimilation. When Samuel Johnson wrote his dictionary in 1755, he was attempting to standardize what had already become an unruly—or gloriously rich—language, infused with new words prompted by British colonization, exploration, and technology. When English came to the new world, it was further expanded by Native American words like *canoe* and *moccasin.* Although English, like French, German, and Italian, has Indo-European roots, its diction is less pure and more interesting because synonyms have roots in both the Anglo-Saxon and the Latinate/Greek, and because it has absorbed new world words. A writer can often choose between these families to achieve a particular effect; *inculcate* and *masticate*, for example, are different from *teach* and *chew.*

Until our era, most writers learned Latin and Greek and had training in the history and structure of English and in etymology. Even William Blake, who was not trained in classical languages, taught himself enough about Latin and Greek to use the devices of etymology in his poems. Times have changed, however. While 41% of high school students study a foreign language, only 1.5% of that group study Latin, much less Greek. Even fewer have any exposure to the history of English. This means that most contemporary readers, like me, must make a conscious effort to learn etymology by looking up words in a dictionary that lists their roots. I've come to rely on this practice while writing my own poems.

The etymology of a word can deepen the meaning of a poem by carrying an image. For instance, the root of *cross* in *crucial* or the root of *star* in *consider*. Understanding word origins helps readers understand their buried or historical meanings as well as see the amplifying images they carry with them. Historical meanings remain in poems like watermarks.

When I'm stuck with a poem, I skim the pages of a print dictionary until I get to a word whose root I didn't know and then insert it. It's like opening a window in a stuffy room; the word history asks me to connect it to what is already on the page and can lead me to a new insight.

While writing my first book, *Red Under the Skin,* I had a group of poems about food, but at that point, none about sweet things, so I read about vanilla in a botany book. The first half of my poem "Creation Story" discusses the growth habit of this climbing orchid alongside its culinary history, but it was etymology that gave me the insight:

> from the Spanish, *vainilla,*
> diminutive of Latin, *vagina,*
> the term for sheath.
> A vagina becomes a case—
> a portico covering travelers,
> a scabbard for a sword—
> the way Ptolemy made the earth the center
> and the Greeks named orchid tubers
> after testicles.
> No matter that some words glide over the tongue,
> entice us with sweet stories,
> we're still stuck
> with their roots in our throats.

The idea that language is invented and then owned by those in power is one of my enduring themes. In my most recent book of poems, *Vivarium,* I compiled words starting with the same letter and then looked up their histories. For the prose poem "P," the phrase *peculiar treasure* in the Bible made me look up *peculiar* which comes from *pecu,* the Latin for *cattle.* The word *peccadillo* refers to a small sin, which led me to *peccare*, Latin for *sin*. The end of the poem synthesizes these ideas:

> our peculiar institution produced slaves worth six
> billion dollars. There's a difference between owning
> human beings and owning cattle. The latter we eat,
> like pecans, from the Cree, *pakan,* that which is
> cracked with a stone. A New World nut, so rich
> in oil, undomesticated until 1846.

Poems must, of course, be well made; no one likes to sit in a chair that wobbles. Using the history of words can strengthen that chair, giving it roots.

Poem and Prompt

Because it looked hotter that way

we let our hair down. It wasn't so much that we
worried about what people thought or about keeping it real
but that we knew this was our moment. We knew we'd blow our cool

sooner or later. Probably sooner. Probably even before we
got too far out of Westmont High and had kids of our own who left
home wearing clothes we didn't think belonged in school.

Like Mrs. C. whose nearly unrecognizably pretty senior photo we
passed every day on the way to Gym, we'd get old. Or like Mr. Lurk
who told us all the time how it's never too late

to throw a Hail Mary like he did his junior year and how we
could win everything for the team and hear the band strike
up a tune so the cheer squad could sing our name, too. Straight

out of a Hallmark movie, Mr. Lurk's hero turned teacher story. We
had heard it a million times. Sometimes he'd ask us to sing
with him, *T-O-N-Y-L-U-R-K Tony Tony Lurk Lurk Lurk. Sin*

ironia, con sentimiento, por favor, and then we
would get back to our Spanish lessons, opening our thin
textbooks, until the bell rang and we went on to the cotton gin

in History. Really, this had nothing to do with being cool. We
only wanted to have a moment to ourselves, a moment before Jazz
Band and after Gym when we could look in the mirror and like it. June

and Tiffany and Janet all told me I looked pretty. We
took turns saying nice things, though we might just as likely say, Die
and go to hell. Beauty or hell. No difference. The bell would ring soon.

—Camille T. Dungy

Dungy's poem uses a form known as a *golden shovel*, invented by poet Terrance Hayes as a tribute to Gwendolyn Brooks. The rules of the form are few and simple:

1. Borrow a line from a poem by Brooks or any other poet.
2. Use each word of the line as the last word in a line of your new poem, going in order from beginning to end.

If you read down the right margin of Dungy's poem, you will find the words of Brooks's "We Real Cool." Because the source poem is short, Dungy borrows all the words, not just one line. Notice that while the words are borrowed, the content and form of her poem are very different. Subject matter and tone may be somewhat reminiscent of the model poem—the passage of Time, nostalgia—but no one would read this poem and recognize its source.

Observe how Dungy often varies the original meaning of a word. *Lurk*, a verb in Brooks's poem, is now a proper noun, the name of a Spanish teacher. *Sin* is now part of a Spanish phrase, *sin ironia*, meaning *without irony*. *Gin* is no longer alcohol but part of the cotton gin. *June* is no longer a month but the name of a girlfriend.

✎ ✎ ✎

Let's do a golden shovel poem. First, find a line you'd like to use. If you want to use a line from a poem by Brooks, her work is readily available online, but remember that you may borrow from another poet as well. Remember also that you may choose to be ambitious and use more than one line. If the poem is short, you may, as Dungy has, use the words of the entire poem.

Write the words down the righthand margin of a piece of paper. Use the same order in which the words appear in your source.

Now let your imagination guide you into a new poem. Focus on the words in front of you, not on the original poem. The goal is not to write something similar or in response to, but to find a new direction.

Explore various connotations and denotations of the end words. See where that takes you.

If you like, you can use a title that runs into your first line as Dungy's does.

Find an appropriate form for your poem. Perhaps three-line stanzas. Perhaps not.

Sample Poems

Family

There was no such thing as spare change. We
didn't ask for pennies for candy. We really
did know the score. If we wanted heat on cool
mornings we needed to bank the fire at night. We
ate what was on our plates; there were no left-
overs. Walked through snow and rain to school.
Arrived on time, mostly, although some days we
dawdled, especially me. I would find a way to lurk
out of site, in an alley, and then get to school late.
Sometimes I look back and wonder how it is we
poor kids made it through. We were strike-
out kings, I suppose. We seemed set to go straight
from school to work for *ASARCO*. But dad fixed that. We
went together to the smelter. His friends would sing
out "Hey, Pal!" I thought he had it made. "It would be a sin,"
he said, "for you to work here. Look at us. We
break our backs shoveling coal. Paycheck too damn thin
to pay our bills. Might as well rub a lamp, expect a *Jinn*
to grant our wishes. You need school. Your mom and I, we
want more for you." He liked country music so I chose jazz.
I didn't know that he would be gone, that year, by June.
The leukemia took him quickly. It seems now that we
barely had him. He was too damned young to die.
You think you have a world of time, but it ends so soon.

—Roy Beckemeyer
published in *River City Poetry*

I Fled

a tribute to William Carlos Williams

> Even so,
the Midwest's long shadow fastens much
faster than you guess, and flight depends
on determination, but the indelible imprint upon
you doesn't evaporate—a stagnant afternoon with a
pop chewing Double Bubble (years before Big Red),
joy never requiring one must be a "big wheel,"
just cut potato eye-chunks and bury in a barrow
while humidity bakes your forehead glazed
and you know after labor reward will come with
squeals, prancing through the squirting Dial-a-Rain
sprinkler's fanning cool fountain of water
as your bare feet prickle from bristling grass beside
the brick steps your parents sit on in front of the
house they built and moved into and painted white,
where one Easter they gave you pink and purple baby chickens.

—Dianne Silvestri

Top Tips: Fifteen Statements about Poetry

—Lee Upton

1. It is often useful to focus on something small—a shell, a coin, a pretzel, a child's bib, the sound and shape of a word—and observe closely. Discovery occurs through concentration, through heightened attention to what may easily be overlooked. The large possibility, the resonant new poem, may enter through a very tiny gate.

2. The poem is smarter than the poet and more rebellious. A strong poem will override its author's initial intentions.

3. A poem stores our secrets—even those secrets we may not know we possess.

4. Poets ought to listen attentively to all the voices around them. And seek out voices they may not have heard before.

5. In your drafts follow your mind wherever it leads, even if the route seems trivial, sentimental, over-heated. Maybe there's something to discover that has been suffocated by dogma, by good intentions, by expectations, by all the ways we have been domesticated.

6. Why should a poem please even a majority of readers or listeners? Perhaps someone needs the particular poem that you wrote. You probably do, at any rate.

7. Turn the poem around to observe its facets—including the history of whatever the poem names.

8. Intelligence is not enough. Cleverness can get in the way. You are feeling your way along a wall in the dark.

9. As we write, the lost people inside us come out to play or pray or lay waste to what terrorizes us.

10. Be patient with the poem and with yourself. You're each wrestling with your creator.

11. Keep your drafts. Lurking among earlier drafts may be the clue you need—or even the true poem, too quickly abandoned.

12. There are poems of praise, poems of rage, poems of mixed emotions, poems that despise emotions emotionally. You have the right to work on a broad canvas, including the right to reject indifference.

13. Frustration can be the signal that you're growing as a writer. One way to write through frustration: assign yourself challenges: a poem with no verbs, a poem with two verbs on every line, a poem that conjures a single color in every stanza without naming the color. While you're focusing on a technical matter, the inner imp who writes all your poems may declare something that you never guessed could be said.

14. Have you ever played hide and seek as a child and no one came to find you? The voice you heard in your head after you realized no one was coming for you—that's poetry.

15. Let's be grateful. We've discovered poetry. We've found a channel into meaning and mystery. We are wildly, wickedly fortunate and should not forget it.

Bonus Prompt: The Dictionary Poem

Choose one of the following words to work with:

arrest
wrinkle
sentence
water
spare
macerate
blossom
arrange
flower
toy

Now get out a good dictionary. Look up your word. Write down all the definitions and synonyms and any information about roots. Note all forms of your word—noun, verb, adjective, adverb. What connotations does your word have? Synonyms? Antonyms? Homonyms?

Use this material to write a new poem. Let your imagination and sense of play get involved. The poem must be more than a dictionary entry.

III. Making Music

Be a songbird, not a parrot.

—Lawrence Ferlinghetti

Craft Tip #7: The Sounds a Poem Can Make

—Marge Piercy

Remember always that poems are composed of sounds and silences. You indicate the silences, the pauses, by where you break the line and by caesuras in the line itself. If you want a more breathless sound, a rush of words, then you carefully break the lines where you do not desire pauses but a run-on style. That moves the poem quickly, whereas many end-stopped lines slow it down.

As a poet, you have many oral resources at your disposal. You can, as Emily Dickinson so often did, create webs of assonance and consonance throughout your poem. I have sometimes diagrammed her poems to enjoy her craft. I have encouraged poets studying with me to do the same. The vowels you choose will slow or speed up the line; the consonant choices can do the same. You watch whether too many s's are creating sounds you don't want. You notice the effect of lots of gutturals.

Of course, rhyme is a common use of sound repetition at the end of lines, but rhyme scattered throughout lines is less sing-songy and can work to enforce the structure of a poem. Slant rhyme, again something Emily Dickinson pioneered, is another way of creating a sound scheme that can enrich a poem

Poems can be made only of sounds without normal coherence, as in Gertrude Stein's poetry. You get an impression, an emotional sense of the poem, but you could not begin to take it apart to drag meaning from it. You enjoy it or you don't. That's it.

Onomatopoeia is a frequent resource. Maybe you're imitating the sound of a motorcycle or a sputtering chop on the grill or a bird or the sound of walking in snow or paddling in water. It's not a bad exercise to try. Even when you're not imitating sounds from the external world, you can make your lines growl, croon, moan, flirt, sing, threaten, cajole. Always be aware of how the lines sound—are you getting the effect you intended or are you at war with your intention?

Repetition is one of the most powerful ways to create memorable verse and a sense of increasing power. It might be simply repeating a word or a phrase, often in a rhythmic way. Incremental repetition ties a poem together and gives an impression of crescendo, of mounting pressure and intensity.

Anaphora, repetition of the same phrase at the beginning of each line, is a common practice in liturgy, but it can also be used to great effect in poetry as in Joy Harjo's "She Had Some Horses." I always tell my poetry students that after they read that particular poem out loud, they'll never forget what the word anaphora means.

It's important to me to always sound out my poems as I'm writing them. For me, the acid test of a poem is the first time I perform it in public. Then I hear where there are unnecessary words, clumps of unaccented syllables that destroy the rhythm of the line, unclear areas, dead spots. That's when I discover if the webs of sound I'm trying to create actually work, if the poem does what I intended it to do. If not, back to work.

The more aware you are of the sound qualities of each poem, the better the poem will perform for an audience. In my poetry workshops, I spend as long on the sound qualities of a poem as I do on imagery, line length, line breaks, stanzas, and the other elements of craft, because the oral elements of a poem are all-important to its effect.

Poem and Prompt

Five to Ten

It snows like a barroom brawl.
After the last punch is thrown,
after the last shard of broken
glass clinks to an otherwise
silent aftermath, the sheriff
nudges the fallen drifters with
the tip of his boot, thankful
that their bluster has gone
to sleep. It snows like a bad
symphony; discordant violins
that sound like the wind
moaning while it assaults
the trees, the senses, and
the small of your back.
It snows like an unfinished
masterpiece. It snows like
a runaway locomotive, like
the makings of an evil
sorcerer's tomb. It snows
like a picture perfect mansion
under construction; jagged
edges, ugly piles of scrap
and danger around every
corner. It snows like a
disease.

—William Greenfield

The title might strike us as enigmatic, but once we read the poem, it makes perfect sense; the poet is referring to the prediction that the storm will drop five to ten inches of snow. Greenfield documents a snowstorm in a series of seven similes.

He begins each simile with *It snows like a*. This anaphora adds force and rhythm to the poem. Read it aloud and you'll feel both. There is only one sentence that does not begin with those words.

In spite of the pattern created by anaphora followed by a simile, there is a good deal of variety in sentence structure. There's an alternation between short and long, simple and elaborate. The first simile is one sentence, one line. The second sentence begins with two subordinate clauses, then introduces the subject, verb, and object of the sentence (*the sheriff / nudges the fallen drifters*). This sentence is the only departure from the pattern of anaphora plus simile, though the two clauses do employ anaphora. This sentence is also the only one that is not a simile but rather an elaboration of the preceding simile.

The second simile contains another simile (thus making an 8th but one not describing the snow) and a list. Then we get a short simile followed by two in one sentence. Simile #6 is an expanded one. The poet ends with the shortest, most powerful simile.

Notice that some of the similes are not strictly logical, e.g., *It snows like an unfinished / masterpiece*. Such fanciful similes add an element of strangeness to the poem, a touch of the surreal.

Notice the diction. Greenfield employs a cluster of words used to describe fighting: the *barroom brawl* of his first simile: *the last punch, fallen drifters, bluster*, and *assaults*.

Finally, notice the form of the poem, how the lines just fall down the page.

✐ ✐ ✐

Let's write a poem in similes. Consider one of the following as your simile starter: *It rains like, It blows like, It sleets like, It floods like, It burns like, It thunders like.*

Give yourself 10 minutes to quickly write a rough draft. Pile up one simile after another. Don't worry about whether they're good or not good, about whether they make sense or not. Don't stop until you have at least ten similes.

Now let's polish it up a bit. Select a strong simile to go first. Select another strong one to go last. Fill in with the others.

Return to the first simile/line/sentence. In the following 6-8 lines develop that simile. Begin with two dependent clauses, both beginning with the same words.

Bring in simile #2 and expand it by including another simile and a list of items in a series.

Then bring in the remaining similes of your choice.

Weave in some diction that pertains to your first simile.

These are some tough tasks here, but worth the effort.

Sample Poems

Divorce Torch

Fire is an event not a thing. Spontaneous
combustion—new love—burns bittersweet
like nightshade—it's toxic and builds without release.

It burns my body
electric, each muscle fiber learns to
scream. The grit of infidelity tears and rips.

There is no salvation here, only long days
of grief, still nights when clouds of insects rise up
apply their sting to the sheen of my mistakes.

It burns like soap—the film of it
licking, spreading red over the white
of my eye.

It burns and bubbles up. Thrusts
through borders, erupts until I lay down
new layers of igneous memories.

Blisters refuse to weep or heal.
My skin peels, sooty with third degree char
years later glares with shiny pink scars.

It burns and spreads like a brush fire, a malignancy
that seeds itself under thorny nodes, builds up
enough heat to sweep my heart clean.

—Jenna Rindo

Gray

it ruins in small unceasing bites as it
swallows winter then spring
snow's purity edged with a dirty fringe
rain's purity collected to a muddy ooze
that sucks or slides

it is more than absence of color

it deceives by promising a silver lining
allows the sun to show
but disallows warmth
it is reality cataracted—light contrived
into auras that flash in a dim world

always it is rain and rain and rain
the worst storms being in the heart
where it sits as soaked despair
dries out as desiccated gloom

it is grief dissolving
from raging dark to almost bearable
it is tarnished silverware
cold, darkening at every edge
yet begging to be caressed
it is moonlight on a meadow
nests of grass beckoning under
calligraphy of tree branches

gray sneaks like a shape-shifter
sets up house
puts up its feet
stays as long as it wants

—Gaye Gambell-Peterson

Craft Tip #8: The Music in the Ore

—Sidney Wade

The sound is the gold in the ore. This, of course, is Robert Frost, from his deeply mysterious and compelling essay, "The Figure a Poem Makes." The reason a poem is a poem, and not prose, in my opinion, is that it sounds a lot better than prose. Yes, prose writers can make beautiful music with their words, but their music is a much subtler thing, strung out over long sentences and pages, and harder to hear than that of a poem. We poets have a whole arsenal of sonic fireworks at our disposal: rhyme, rhythm, alliteration, assonance, half- slant- and near-rhymes, among many others, and we should by all means be using them. When you listen to a poem by B. H. Fairchild, or Randall Mann, or Kay Ryan, for example, you hear, in different versions, mastery of sonics at work. Fairchild's music comes from his wide knowledge and supple usage of our traditional English verse and the Christian liturgy, which is obvious in his gorgeous blank verse lines. Mann's powerful sonic play more often involves rhyme and tightly crafted stanzaic forms, and Ryan's work is simply full to bursting with music.

One way to focus on the music of your work is to discover your own personal rhythm. I'm convinced we each have one, and it's worthwhile trying to find it. My own is dactylic (˘ ˘ ′), as is obvious in my poem, "Shore," which begins *Drenched in the light and seduced by the brilliant green lie of the...* I discovered this one morning by allowing my words to come pouring out, without any conscious artistic meddling, as I pondered the incident that inspired the poem.

Much of that poem, actually, came to me through this exercise: What you do is to pick a topic and get as many words on the page as you can on the subject without censoring yourself at all. Just let 'er rip. You may find your own rhythm is more trochaic, or iambic, as opposed to my own kind of natural moseying lope.

Another way to pay attention to the sound of your words is to train yourself to prune out every single unnecessary word.

Here's an easy one—*that*. I find I am helpless in the face of this humble little word—it finds its way into absolutely everything I write—emails, poems, scholarly papers—and I have to methodically weed it out of everything I write before anyone else sees it. *I told my mother that I was going out* means exactly the same thing as *I told my mother I was going out*. So checking on each word to make sure it is absolutely necessary to the meaning of your poem is a good way to train yourself to constantly pay attention to every single word, to weigh its sound and meaning against the whole, which will make all the words sound a little cleaner and clearer in your own ears, and therefore, of course, in those of the reader.

I have been working for several years now in a form I call the *skinny line*. What I find in working with this narrow little line, mostly in couplets, is that the sheer brevity of the line forces you to be more careful with the sounds you make. When you have such limited space, you have to take advantage of all available sonic possibilities. It is the sound of the words that leads me on, more often than not, when I'm trying to figure out where to go in a poem. Sometimes, once I have laid down a line or two, and have confidence in every one of the words, I look into the rhyming dictionary for all reasonable rhymes, and sometimes surprising new venues are opened as I try to figure out how to use some of the more interesting and/or unusual rhymes provided there.

On the few occasions when I'm not working in the skinny line, I prefer writing in formal structures. The great gift form gives us is this: The requirements of rhyme and meter more often than not force us to come up with new and surprising word choices, line endings, directions, because the sounds need attention and affirmation. In short, listening carefully and artfully to the sound of your words helps mightily in the formation and development of a poem.

Poem and Prompt

April Incantation

O wrathful rain roll down
and down. Outwit the drains,

unground us. Wind and thunder,
steer the torrent's train and throw

us under. Upriver, water, rage
and rack the dam to shatter. Blast

the happy poppies. Let petal-
blood trouble the flooded field.

Crack new bourns and boundaries
into parceled plots. Wreck even

the season that reared you: lick
the lilacs into sobbing heaps.

Flounce the furrows and swallow
the seeds. Gut the leaf-

rucked gutters. Wrestle reed
beds into rags. Wrench up head-

stones, grub the graves and spit
the picked bones in the ocean.

Show us nothing's sacred,
nothing safe. Fair enough. I fed

this flood. I'll take my place
among the fallen sodden.

—Maggie Dietz

An incantation is a chant, a magical song, or a series of words spoken in a rhythmical way so as to create a particular effect. An incantation often has a mesmerizing or hypnotic effect on the listener. As her speaker calls on April's rain to pour down, Dietz relies heavily on musical strategies.

Notice, first of all, the reliance on iambic feet, e.g., *O wrathful rain roll down / and down. Outwit the drains.* These first two lines are perfect iambic trimeter; each line has six syllables with the stress on every second syllable, thus three feet in each line. The pacing of the stressed syllables creates a drum-like effect.

Notice, too, the use of strong verbs—and lots of them: *Flounce, swallow, rage, blast, crack, wreck.* These also contribute to the poem's rhythm.

Another strategy is the predominance of monosyllabic words, a strategy that assaults the ear with a boom, boom, boom.

Then we also find a good deal of alliteration: *Flounce and furrows* and *swallow / the seeds; bourns and boundaries; wreck, wrestle, wrench; grub the graves.* Notice how often Dietz pairs up her words. This adds to the rhythm and to the cumulative power of rain.

The poet also relies on assonance. Note, for example, the repetition of the *uh* sound in *blood trouble the flooded field* and in *Gut the leaf-rucked gutters.*

Another forceful note is sounded with the use of imperative sentences. A direct address is made in line 1 to the *wrathful rain.* Thereafter, each new sentence begins with its verb and *you* is understood.

When we get close to the end of the poem, Dietz pulls a switch, changing from *us* to *I.* With this change, the poem moves to a different level, a more personal one. The speaker now says, *I fed // this flood. I'll take my place / among the fallen sodden.* Both the switch and the words surprise the reader and provoke curiosity. We know that the speaker has cried hard, but not why.

For your own incantation, choose a season, a month, a holiday, a day of the week, or perhaps something associated with one of those, e.g., snow, wind, daffodils.

Brainstorm a list of strong verbs, ones relevant to your choice of topic, e.g., if your topic is winter, your list might include *hail, blast, blow, drift, freeze.*

Begin your draft with a direct address, speaking directly to your topic and as part of a collective, i.e., using *us/we.* Then keep on going. Implore and order. Do not stop to judge or evaluate as you write. Let momentum build up. Let your words tumble out fast and furious.

When you've filled up a page or feel that you've maxed out, bring in a turn. Switch from *us* to *I,* now speaking for yourself rather than for the collective. Or perhaps you'd rather take a different kind of risk. Whatever it is, let it surprise you.

As you revise, be sure to employ some of the same musical strategies used by Dietz: iambic feet, strong verbs, monosyllabic words, alliteration, assonance, imperative sentences.

Sample Poems

Solstice: Mississippi Invocation

Come, green, fill our veins
    with tendrils and broad lobed leaves,
        wave as the rain approaches, teach us
      the secret of swoon, exhaustion. Come,
great-petaled magnolias, scrotal figs
    in the crooks of branches, scarlet bells
        of Carolina creeper, bruised gardenias,
      mosses and lichens that fur the bark of
oaks. Come, fungi, come, buzzards,
    this teeming   is death   is teeming,
        the walls of our houses, the doors
      of our senses, dampen and soften.
Plunge us into sleep and deliquescence,
    we are sap and vine and solstice,
        ooze us, rot us, make us hot and hotter.
      Jasmine, wisteria, twine us, ensnare us,
stupefy us with your sugary blossoms.

—Ann Fisher-Wirth

Anniversary

Oh aching day, go choke
on your familiar tune,

that endless replay of
the strata of our loss.

Your orbit is a curse,
a comet spewing ice,

your annual return
predictable as rust.

Catch a passing freight
or hitchhike down the pike,

the wake of your exhaust
dead weeds along the way.

Go find another home
and sink a garden there,

feed funeral bouquets
for mourners everywhere.

No scent of roses gone
or blood from sudden thorn

can thrust me into arms
that once again are gone.

—Penny Harter

Craft Tip #8: Writing a Descriptive List Poem

—Pattiann Rogers

Putting a list together in a poetic way can be engaging and enjoyable. The skills learned and perfected in writing a list poem can also be helpful when writing any type of poem. The most common and simplest list is primarily descriptive, composed of single words or short phrases, and perhaps a complete sentence or two, to prevent a monotony of sound.

Any list poem nearly always evolves into a celebration, no matter the subject. This is a descriptive list poem of mine that may illustrate that thought, and it also provides examples of the suggestions about writing one that I'll be offering.

Geocentric

Indecent, self-soiled, bilious
reek of turnip and toadstool
decay, dribbling the black oil
of wilted succulents, the brown
fester of rotting orchids,
in plain view, that stain
of stinkhorn down your front,
that leaking roil of bracket
fungi down your back, you
purple-haired, grainy-fuzzed
smolder of refuse, fathering
fumes and boils and powdery
mildews, enduring the constant
interruption of sink-mire
flatulence, contagious
with ear wax, corn smut,
blister rust, backwash
and graveyard debris, rich
with manure bog and dry-rot
harboring not only egg-addled
garbage and wrinkled lip
of orange-peel mold but also

the clotted breath of overripe
radish and burnt leek, bearing
every dank, malodorous rut
and scarp, all sulphur fissures
and fetid hillside seepages, old,
old, dependable, engendering
forever the stench and stretch
and warm seeth of inevitable
putrefaction, nobody
loves you as I do.

To begin a descriptive list poem, pick a subject that you're interested in and really like and that has a large vocabulary associated with it. The more words you have to choose from in composing your descriptive list, the better. The subject can be something outdoors or indoors, a single tree, a river bank, the contents of a child's toy chest, a road disappearing over a hill, a scene of weather, anything.

The first three or four items in your list will introduce the subject and probably set the tone/voice of the poem—serious, humorous, casual, stern, angry, afraid. Consider those first descriptive words carefully.

Listen to the music of the words as you begin to put them in an order. Music is the most crucial component of the list poem. Because your descriptive list is simply a lyrical list, it won't be constrained by logic or narrative or even meaning, and because you have a generous vocabulary to choose from, you possess the freedom to select your vowels and consonants and place them where they help to create the music. Use all the craft tools you have—alliteration and assonance, rhymes and half rhymes.

A cadence will develop as you put the words together. Write awhile and then read out loud what you've written. Are you satisfied with the cadence and sound as to tone and beat? If not, try a different arrangement of words, always reading out loud. You want your reader (and you are your own first reader) to *feel* the poem, and this must happen in the body through the music of the language, the stressed and unstressed syllables, the hard consonants and the soft ones, the silence and spaces.

You can use commas for short rests, line breaks or dashes for pauses. As poet, you should hear and feel this music and detect when it falters, then you can rewrite to correct that faltering line or section. The music will help you in selecting your words. Listen.

Depending on the tone of the poem, an unexpected item in the list, a surprise, can heighten interest. Adding a complete sentence somewhere in the poem can serve as a break in the music and enrich the poem.

Try to intuit when to stop the list and to begin the ending. You won't want to tire your reader with a list that's too long and loses momentum, or disappoint by stopping too soon.

Watching for all of these suggestions can't happen at once, of course. Many drafts and rewrites will be necessary. But that's the fun of it, putting together the pieces of the beautiful, musical puzzle that you're creating.

Watch, feel, and listen to the poem as you write. Loosen your control on it a little now and then, and let your list show you the direction it's going. The music, the beat, the cadence will help you with this, too. Once you get a few lines established, the descriptive list poem may almost write and conclude itself.

Poem and Prompt

What Some Things Are Worth According to Her Grandfather

Any job worth doing is worth doing right.
And any right worth having is worth

a fight. Remember, though, fighting
like cats and dogs is for the birds, while a bird

in the BBQ pit is worth two in the bush.
And any bush worth beating around

is worth its weight in glitter, even though
all that glitters is not worth a penny.

Gee, how many times have I told you,
a penny for your thoughts—

well, that's just worth bull (but not the kind
of bull that goes off half-cocked

like a gun in a china shop.) Speaking of shopping,
shopping is therapy but only if you learn to say no,

because no one's island is worth a stick in your eye.
A stick in your eye, ya say? Don't forget:

An eye for an eye pulls the whole world up by the roots.
And everyone knows the root of all evil has no secrets.

Besides, a secret's only worth keeping
if it's as pretty as a picture, since a picture sells

a thousand stories, and a good story makes the world
blow up. Surely, what goes up must be worth

double time and time is money, so take that fork
in the wall. Yes, walls have ears, but no voice

to spill the beans. And a hill of beans
is just one thing after another. But another needle

in the haystack, well, now that's worth a second look.
Of course, what looks and quacks like a duck

is the wrong man for the job! And we all know
any job worth doing is worth doing right.

—Nancy Chen Long

Titles matter as this one illustrates. It's quirky and therefore
quickly grabs the reader's attention. It also sets a direction for
the poem and gives purpose to its list; the title helps the poem
make sense.

Note the dexterity and playfulness of this poem, its cleverness
and its humor. It consists of a list of pieces of advice given to
the speaker by her grandfather. These items are expressed as
common expressions, maxims, and clichés, all refurbished by
being misquoted and combined with other expressions.

Notice what Long does with repetition. First, she takes one
word from the title—*worth*—and repeats it in line 1's expression:
Any job worth doing is worth doing right. That same word
then appears twice in line 2 and is repeated numerous times
thereafter. Almost every stanza repeats some word twice, e.g.,
stanza 2 repeats *bird*, stanza 3 repeats *bush*, and so on. The
poet also often repeats a word from one stanza in the next, e.g.,
penny appears in stanza 4, then again in stanza 5. Repetition
continues throughout the poem. Sometimes just one word gets
repeated, sometimes an entire phrase as in stanza 8 where we
have *because no one's island is worth a stick in your eye. / A
stick in your eye, ya say?*

Notice the slang *ya say* in the preceding quotation and the earlier *Gee* of stanza 5. This casual diction is augmented by the use of parentheses, a dash, and an exclamation point. Small matters, but they contribute to a distinctive voice.

Long also uses rhyme effectively. Notice how stanza 1 is braided into the second stanza with the rhyme of *right* and *fight*. Such rhymes weave their way throughout the poem. Another rhyming device is near rhymes, e.g., *well, bull, pulls, all, sells, wall, spill, hill.* Scattered throughout the poem, these words make a lovely series of echoes.

Finally, notice the last stanza: *And we all know / any job worth doing is worth doing right.* Thus, the poet returns to the beginning of the poem, completing a nice circle.

✐ ✐ ✐

For your own list poem, come up with a title similar to Long's, for example:

> The Facts of Life According to His Gym Teacher
> My Mother Tells Me What Matters
> Father's Life Lessons Freely Offered
> My Twin's Cranky List of Complaints

Before you begin your draft, compile a list of common expressions. Here are some possibilities to choose from, but feel free to supplement with others.

> What doesn't kill you makes you stronger.
> What goes up must come down.
> Early to bed and early to rise makes a man healthy,
>   wealthy, and wise.
> A picture is worth a thousand words.
> Nip this in the bud.
> Spare the rod, spoil the child.
> A stitch in time saves nine.
> Sticks and stones may break my bones, but words
>   will never hurt me.
> Don't make a mountain out of a molehill.

Kill the chicken to scare the monkey.
Dumb as a box of rocks
Like a warm biscuit on a Sunday morning
The elephant in the room

Begin your draft, as Long does, with a common expression consisting of one sentence. Include in that sentence one word from your title. Remember to repeat that word throughout your poem.

Continue with your next expression and fuse it with another. You may or may not repeat and change some of the expressions as you go on.

Use some of the other techniques of repetition used by Long. Try repeating a word from one stanza in the next stanza. Try repeating a word twice in one line or in a stanza. Try repeating an entire phrase.

Join some stanzas with rhyme, taking a word from one stanza and rhyming it in the next, not necessarily at line endings. Also include some near rhymes and weave them throughout the poem.

Insert some colloquial words at the beginning of sentences. Or you might go in the opposite direction and use formal, eloquent utterances.

End your poem with a repetition of your poem's first line.

Sample Poems

My Aunt Betty Says She's Nothing But Ordinary

I'm nothing but ordinary—merely average.
Certainly never been a status seeker;

for sure, some days I could scarcely be
any meeker. Never the bee's knees

or the high wire act,
the crème de la crème,

or the renowned fat cat.
By no means topnotch—

not top of the charts either.
Never billed as first-rate or top banana,

in no way the kingpin
or needing VIP status.

I've never led a cause,
never been a mover

or a shaker—
haven't turned any heads

or been a headline maker.
Most things I've done have been

nothing to write home about.
I entertain no grand illusion

of first class status. On a map of
the two Antilles Islands,

I'd no doubt be the lesser
and when it comes to star-gazing—

label me Ursa Minor, not Major.
I'll never rattle the rafters

or blow the lid off the kettle,
never win the blue ribbon

or wear the gold medal.
I've never raised a major ruckus,

nor caused commotion or a scene,
just lived an ordinary life

that's been fairly routine.
I'm not a maven, or a master,

not a bigwig, a top chef or big shot.
I'm not anywhere near a big deal.

I'm merely mediocre, so-so, they say,
commonplace and down-to-earth.

I'm a-dime-a-dozen, no great shakes,
never any need to take a big bow,

just your run-of-the-mill, everyday
nothing but ordinary, middling kind of a gal.

—Kim Klugh

Aunt Glenna Lays Down the Law

A chicken lays eggs, you lie in bed too long.
Children should be seen and not heard.

A bird in the hand is worth two in the pie.
You're a bull in a china shop.

Oh, Patsy, can't you do ANYTHING right?

If you can't say anything nice,
don't say it twice.

If you lie, your nose will grow.
Keep your ducks all in a row.

Stupid is as stupid does.
How can you be so dumb?

Lay your troubles down.
Don't lay all your eggs in one basket.

Say thank you, say please.
Money doesn't grow on trees.

Be sweet, be smart, be better.
Be somebody!

A stitch in time saves nine hundred.
Witty women catch the early worm.

Busy hands stay out of trouble.
Don't be late. Sit up straight.

ELBOWS OFF THE TABLE!

Bread crusts will make your hair curl.
Clean your plate.

Say thank you, say please.
Your face will freeze that way.

Seize the hen, seize the hour.
Early to bed, early to rise

makes a girl pretty, witty, and wise.
Never trust a woman.

The early bird swallows the worm.
Everything you do is wrong.

You lie like Pinocchio.
A chicken lays eggs, you lie in bed too long.

—Patricia Fargnoli

Top Tips: Ten Things about Poetry

—Patricia Smith

1. Every day, do this: Sit in a quiet chair in a quiet room. Close your eyes. Draw in a breath and hold it. Eventually you'll hear a sound that rumbles up through the floorboards, climbs the walls, shudders the rafters. When the din reaches an impossible crescendo, you'll know one thing for sure. You are living your life out loud. You are a relentless witness. You have what it takes to write poetry.

2. Ten pages a day. TEN PAGES A DAY. Stop the sighing, get those eyes back in your head. I don't mean ten pages of perfect poetry, or ten pages of revision, or ten pages of new sparkly stuff. I mean ten pages *toward your art*. For instance, if you're writing a poem set in the antebellum South and you take three pages of notes to strengthen the backdrop of said poem, those three notes count as three of the ten. If you see a wacky newspaper headline and know there's a poem in there somewhere, and you scribble a page or two of possibilities, that page or two counts as one or two of the ten.

3. The ten pages are *non-negotiable*. Even if you drag yourself in at 3 a.m. after a night of dancing yourself raw. Even if you've spent all day going 'round and 'round on the itty It's A Small World gondola at Disney with three perpetually puking toddlers. Even if you've been teaching middle school all day, or bagging groceries all day or greeting customers at Walmart's front entrance all day or sitting on your butt all day. Your work for the day is not done until those TEN (not eight, not nine-and-three-quarters) are done. Look at it this way—you can't leave your 9-to-5 at 2 p.m. after telling the boss, "I just didn't have it in me today." Your poetry is just that kind of commitment. It's your reminder that what you are doing is *not* a recreational activity. It is your J-O-B.

4. Discover one new poet every week. Scan the bookshelves, scour the web, hike it to a poetry reading even though you don't recognize a single name on the bill. Discover the good *and* the

bad—try to figure out what the bad are *trying* to do and why they're failing so barely or so spectacularly. Remember every bad is good to someone. And every good should strive for better.

5. Read as much poetry as you can. I'm addicted to lit journals, because I can open one and sample from all realms of the canon. Lit journals are like little literary amusement parks. Subscribe to the ones you like, hit the library (that's a big building with lots of books inside, and you can take the books *home!*) for the others.

Both you and I know that poets are, by far, the most talented of writers—we take sloppy, unwieldy stories and tuck them into tight, exquisitely controlled spaces. Poets are the best thing ever, and poetry is even better than that. But it's okay to go slumming and read fiction, CNF, plays, etc. Lately, it all wants to be poetry anyway.

6. Listen to as much poetry as you can. There's nothing like going to an actual reading to hear actual poets read their actual poetry from an actual stage. But if you hate gatherings, have a metaphor allergy, or live in Bugtussle, Kentucky (where even Billy Collins has yet to venture), there are still plenty of online paths to those dulcet tones. For example, in the Library of Congress's online Archive of Recorded Poetry and Literature, you can hear readings by Gwendolyn Brooks (our Ms. Brooks should be *require*d listening), Robert Frost, Derek Walcott, Audre Lorde, Jack Gilbert, Lucille Clifton. Luckily for those of us who write, read, study, love or obsess over poetry, no poet's voice is ever lost.

7. Ya need dogs. DOGS. Nebelungs, parakeets, ferrets, Siamese fighting fish, howler monkeys, hamsters, lizards, or sugar gliders are all decidedly sub-par when it comes to finding and becoming besties with, your ideal writing companion. Look at it this way: When you're weep-sweating over the seventh revision of that weighty sestina (the one that will be due an hour ago), and your nuclear family and so-called friends have abandoned you simply because your eyes are a little wild and you've forgone elements of hygiene, only a canine will remain at your side, kissing you randomly and doing that cute head tilt thing

when you scream. My dog Rondo is a master of caesura placement. Brady the Berner keeps my line breaks honest. He's a diehard formalist, a bit of a snob.

8. Learn meter. Master forms. Even if you break out in hives at the sight of a dactyl, even if you're 100% certain that you will never pen a sonnet or tackle hendecasyllabics, you will never regret having that knowledge in your toolbox. Remember that poem you've been carrying around in various stages of feverish revision, and for some reason it's—*just not working?* Sometimes that's because the poem is asking for something you do not yet know how to do. For instance, that piece with the muted, but resounding repetition? Maybe it wants to be a pantoum or a villanelle. Maybe you need to commit wholly to anaphora. (And no, that's not the name of your mother's hairdresser.) It's all about giving your poems a chance to tell you what they want to be—and being able to answer.

9. Resist categorization. For years, I was a slammer. Then I was a spoken word poet. Then I was an urban poet, a feminist, a cultural commentator. The problem was that none of those designations came from me. I am most comfortable with the label *storyteller*, because it doesn't imply borders. If someone tells you that you're something often enough, there's a danger in becoming just that. Never write or read to anyone else's specifications.

10. Ask yourself: *If there were no possibility of publication, no audience, no accolades or exposure whatsoever, would I still be writing poetry?* If the answer is no, the good news is that you can turn back to your semblance of a life at any time. If your answer is yes, congratulations. You've signed on for numbing doubt, envy, heartbreak, incessant stress, dimming confidence, and confounding obsession. You realize that poetry is not a recreational exercise. It's a breathing. It's a responsibility. It's the out loud your life is meant to live.

Bonus Prompt: The Chant Poem

Begin your first line with *I believe*. Complete the thought, then keep going. Begin each new line with the same phrase. Keep going for 15-20 lines. Write rapidly.

Go back and either delete 2-3 *I believe* phrases (keeping the rest of each line), or insert 2-3 new lines that do not use *I believe*.

Keep in mind that pattern is good, but too much pattern becomes predictable and tiresome. It encourages the reader to skim read. Set up your pattern, then break it. Joe Brainard does this in his famous poetic memoir, *I Remember*. Again and again he begins a sentence with *I remember,* but just when we expect another repetition, he surprises us, e.g., *I remember the only time I ever saw my mother cry. I was eating apricot pie*. His first sentence pursues the pattern of repetition; the second sentence breaks the pattern.

Read your poem aloud and notice the musical effect of the anaphora.

Other starter phrases for another day:

> I want
> Because I could not
> I wish
> Forgive me if
> I remember
> He broke

IV. Working with Sentences and Line Breaks

As I altered my syntax, I altered my intellect.

—W. B. Yeats

Craft Tip #10: The Music of the Sentences

—Molly Peacock

Poets are always concerned about the line. But the line only provides one type of music in the poem. Here is a craft tip from a poet who also writes prose: Pay attention to the music of the sentence. If you want to shake up a tired poem, vary the sentence structure! The varieties of sentences have huge rhythmic effects.

1. Simple sentences

Here's Emily Dickinson's simple declarative sentence in poem 611: *I see thee better—in the dark.* A simple subject-verb-object sentence—with a devastating prepositional phrase as a punchline.

2. Exclamations

An exclamatory sentence changes the color of the emotional palette of the poem. Poets are often taught not to use the exclamation point, but, used sparingly, they can be effective. Listen to the lilt in Frank O'Hara's voice in *Lunch Poems:*

> Leaf! You are so big!
> How can you change your
> color, then just fall!
>
> As if there were no
> such thing as integrity!

3. Commands

Invite instructions into the poem, the way John Donne does in "The Canonization" when his speaker says, *For God's sake hold your tongue, and let me love*, then later gives out these edicts:

> Take you a course, get you a place,
>   Observe his honor, or his grace,
> Or the king's real, or his stampèd face
>   Contemplate; what you will, approve,
>   So you will let me love.

You could do worse than take a tip from the seventeenth century.

4. Fragments

Most poets use fragments. But do you dare to use ellipses? I had to turn to them in *The Analyst*. The linked poems in that book are about my 40-year relationship with my analyst, and how it continued in a new form after my analyst's stroke caused her to close her practice. The whole book is about psychoanalysis and poetry—and pauses. There's the pausing as a patient speaks, of course, but also the pausing of the analyst's practice after her stroke. My former analyst pauses many times in her conversations now, since it is difficult for her to remember certain words. In this poem, "Speaking of Painting and Bird Watching," a painter, Katie Kinsky, and I are talking about huge trees in front of her house while, at the same time, I am thinking about how my analyst was felled.

> "If someone chain-sawed my big trees,"
> Katie said, "I could never paint the stumps
> like those fancy-asses who draw them
> just for the design..."

5. Compound sentences

These, too, can be useful, especially ones with that deliciously ignorable conjunction, *and*. Be not afraid of the *and*; it means you are thinking. Why not be a poet with a mind that links what others might think is the unlinkable?

I believe in being killed, and I believe in poetry. That's one line that is also a compound sentence in a poem called "Credo" from *The Analyst*.

6. Complex sentences

These can add a level of sophistication to the poem, especially those that introduce time into the poem, with such words as *after, when, before, since, during, whenever,* and the savory *yet*. These are the little words that a workshop can talk you out of because they may feel extra—but don't listen! These seemingly insignificant words are the language of thought because they add sequence and conditionality to what you are saying. Actually elucidating the steps of your thought process in a poem can be a revelation both to you and to your reader. Afraid what you've thought is too obvious? Think again, you smart person. Your thought process is unique to you; to follow the steps of your associations is a pleasure to a reader. What seems obvious to you might even surprise you.

The first line, which is also the first sentence, of "The Argument," by A. E. Stallings, begins with *After*. Stallings follows this with another complex sentence, and she ends her quatrain with a simple sentence.

> After the argument, all things were strange.
> They stood divided by their eloquence
> Which had surprised them after so much silence.
> Now there were real things to rearrange.

7. Questions

Here's Marilyn Nelson's poem "Balance," where the speaker poses a question about Master Taylor, the slave owner of Diverne. The query interrupts the flow of the narrative—and enriches it.

> What might explain the metamorphosis
> he underwent when she paraded by
> with tea-cakes, in her fresh and shabby dress?

Questions can also rough up the texture in a too-smooth, over-revised poem, don't you think?

Poem and Prompt

On the Sadness of Wedding Dresses

On starless, windless nights like this
I imagine
I can hear the wedding dresses
Weeping in their closets,
Luminescent with hopeless longing,
Like hollow angels.
They know they will never be worn again.
Who wants them now,
After their one heroic day in the limelight?
Yet they glow with desire
In the darkness of closets.
A few lucky wedding dresses
Get worn by daughters—just once more,
Then back to the closet.
Most turn yellow over time,
Yellow from praying
For the moths to come
And carry them into the sky.
Where is your mother's wedding dress,
What closet?
Where is your grandmother's wedding dress?
What, gone?
Eventually they all disappear,
Who knows where.
Imagine a dump with a wedding dress on it.
I saw one wedding dress, hopeful at Goodwill.
But what sad story brought it there,
And what sad story will take it away?
Somewhere a closet is waiting for it.
The luckiest wedding dresses
Are those of wives
Betrayed by their husbands
A week after the wedding.

They are flung outside the double-wide,
Or the condo in Telluride,
And doused with gasoline.
They ride the candolescent flames,
Just smoke now,
Into a sky full of congratulations.

—James Galvin

Galvin's poem is reminiscent of Pablo Neruda's "Ode to Socks." The form is similar as is the use of first person point of view. But while Neruda's poem praises the socks, Galvin's poem bemoans the sorrow of wedding dresses. Thus, his poem is a kind of reverse ode, one rich with irony as he attaches sadness to what is ordinarily associated with joy. He even refers to the dresses of brides betrayed by their husbands within a week of marriage as the "luckiest dresses."

Notice the poet's use of personification. The dresses weep, long, know, and pray. Galvin also uses metonymy, that is, the dresses represent the brides. Consider how the use of these two figures evokes an emotional response from the reader.

Questions play a significant role in the poem, coming to a total of five. These questions make us feel spoken to. They command our attention and compel us to think.

Galvin also makes ample use of imagery. He effectively contrasts light and dark images. For example, it's on dark nights that the speaker can hear the dresses weeping, *Luminescent with hopeless longing*. Our pity is evoked as we are asked to imagine the one dress thrown ignominiously on top of a dump, another one at Goodwill, and the ones that get tossed outside, doused in gasoline, and sent out in *candolescent flames*.

Notice, as you read the poem aloud, how prevalent the long *o* sound is in such words as *hopeless, hollow, know, heroic, glow, yellow, over, those, condo, smoke*. This use of assonance adds a mournful sound to the poem.

For your own ironic ode, think of a group of items that might be praised, e.g., shoes, sweaters, hats, cookies, chocolates. Choose one. Then instead of praising the items in your category, express a different emotion such as anger, regret, disgust, jealousy, pity. Alternatively, you might want to select a single item.

Use first person point of view and be conscious of a reader/auditor, occasionally speaking directly to that person or persons.

Try your hand at the techniques Galvin employs:

1. A setting that ignites the speaker's thoughts

2. Personification and/or metonymy

3. Questions

4. Images, especially at the end of your poem

5. Assonance—choose a single vowel sound to echo throughout your poem. Work on this during revision.

Sample Poems

On the Sadness of Sweaters

after James Galvin

On the thick summer mornings
when heat seeps into each
corner, each crease, I can hear
the sweaters sighing. They are
stored in cedar chests, sleeves
folded toward torso, a faint
stain of smoke lingers along the hem.

Some sweaters weep, contained
in strange plastic boxes, lids are
locked against moths, against
light, then slid under beds like
the dirty magazines my brother
slipped between mattress and box spring.

Soon these sweaters are filled
with undiagnosed shame. The tag
on the seam boasting wool or cashmere
material fades away. Caustic sweat
stored in each armpit from interviews gone
wrong reek in the brew of summer heat.

The sweaters dream of harvest moons,
chilly nights, shoulder to shoulder around
a campfire. Guitar picks and candy
apple lipsticks wait to be pulled from deep
pockets. Long sleeves yearn to be tugged
over fingers, wait to be blessed with necessity.

—Jenna Rindo

Waiting for the Salvation Army

She stands naked and dusty
in the dark, but utters
no recrimination. Silence
her specialty. She looks smaller
now that the books and files
which used to keep her warm
have been removed and all
her cracks and scars and scratches
are visible. I might have
loved her for her place
of origin, my grandmother's
living room. She kept
some of my grandmother's
paperweights and postcards. I might
have loved her for her ample
drawers and built-in compartments.
But I did not, even though
she was where I'd go
to share my deepest secrets.
I never massaged her
with mineral oil. I rarely wiped
her leather and mahogany top.
To me she became one more burden,
one more thing acquired
by circumstance rather than choice.
It's time for her to go.
If she cares, she will not say so.

—Jessica de Koninck

Craft Tip #11: Syntax: The Life Force of Poems

—Anne Marie Macari

Syntax is one of the least talked about yet most useful ways to bring energy into a poem. Syntax simply means the order our words take in our poems. If the word *syntax* makes you think of grammar and grammar makes you nervous, try thinking of it more simply. Words in some kind of order. Ordered words. Ways to arrange words. Words as arrangements on the page. Arranging words a poem is made. I was once a word-arranger and wandered through sentences. You get the idea.

Most of us have some kind of fallback grammatical order that we use without thinking, a way of putting a line on the page. The danger of that is predictability within the poem and from poem to poem. A predictable syntax can kill the mystery; it will keep the poem static.

"The Snow Man," by Wallace Stevens, is a fifteen-line poem that is one long, drawn-out sentence. The poet keeps us reading, pulling us deeper into the freezing landscape, building his poem line by line, image by image, drawing the sentence out and not letting the reader *arrive* anywhere.

> One must have a mind of winter
> To regard the frost and the boughs
> Of the pine-trees crusted with snow;
>
> And have been cold a long time
> To behold the junipers shagged with ice,
> The spruces rough in the distant glitter
>
> Of the January sun; and not to think
> Of any misery in the sound of the wind,
> In the sound of a few leaves,
>
> Which is the sound of the land
> Full of the same wind
> That is blowing in the same bare place

For the listener, who listens in the snow,
And, nothing himself, beholds
Nothing that is not there and the nothing that is.

The poem feels longer than it is, it feels circular with its repetitions, and even when we do arrive at the ending the poem continues unspooling inside us. In that one long sentence "The Snow Man" evokes existential questions. The speaker/reader stands alone in the forbidding landscape beholding *Nothing that is not there and the nothing that is.*

If we look at another iconic American poem, one most of us have been familiar with since school, we can find multiple levels of meaning in its syntax. If Stevens' poem is about mystery, about drawing out thought until it seems to unravel into the *Nothing that is not there*, then Gwendolyn Brooks's "We Real Cool" is all about brevity. The poem begins, *We real cool. We / Left school. We // Lurk late.* Suppose Brooks had instead written "We are really cool / We left school and lurk late into the night"? In other words, suppose her syntax were more ordinary? No doubt we would not all know this poem.

Short lines, short sentences, short stressed words, couplets that rhyme internally so they also evoke brevity and closure—all these support and heighten the impact of the last truncated line: *Die soon.* With her periods mid-line, Brooks offers up a syncopated rhythm, a music that we feel in the bodies of the boy-men, but it's not the drawn-out philosophical music of the Stevens' poem. It's a lively music, a strong pulse—but it can't last. The music and their lives are played out almost before they can begin. That tragedy is felt in large measure because of syntax, the unusually tight and sharp-pointed composition of the poem.

There are so many ways to say something. A poem needs to find its particular music, and syntax is crucial to that sound. Meaning is made in the details. A poem's music is not only about consonants and vowels touching each other in interesting ways, it's also about sentences or fragments, verbs or missing verbs, articles or no articles. It's about not starting every line in the same way. Leaning toward strange rather than predictable. It's about understanding that the unit of measure is not the sentence; that the sentence is in service to the line, as Stevens and Brooks so beautifully show us. In rearranging our words, in taking out or putting in, we are guiding ourselves deeper into the poem, discovering what more there is to say. At our best we are deep-making, we are calling something through us to the page with an alert ear, however subconsciously, to syntax.

Syntax is a kind of code in the poem, the patterns the poet must discover each time she engages with all that infinity, all the words and all the ways the words can be strung together, to write her one-off, her poem with no twin, calling it out of its dream state and onto the page.

Poem and Prompt

The Joy-Bringer

breaks the light through the oak leaves at dawn.
The joy-bringer injects the red bird's red.
The joy-bringer brings the green, lets the cup runneth over
into a saucer, from which you can sip.
Gives fish the river, and the river the fish.
If by two inches you avoid a piano
falling on your head
and later at the hospital fall in love with the doctor
who removes a few splinters
of ivory and black piano lacquer
from your left calf: the joy-bringer
arranged that. Also the chilled artesian water
spilling from a pipe only two inches above the ground,
from which you drank on your hands and knees,
on a few boards or branches, you bowed in the muck and drank
that sweet cold reaching-up.
You drank among the skunk cabbage, ferns, a small brook
at your back: again, guess what,
the joy-bringer! In fact, let us praise
the joy-bringer for these seven
things: 1) right lung, 2) left lung, 3) heart, 4) left brain,
5) right brain, 6) tongue, 7) the body to put them in.
Thank you, joy-bringer!
And thanky, thanky too for just-mown hay
cut an inch from its roots
to bleed its perfume into the air!

—Thomas Lux

Lux's title runs into the first line of the poem and serves as the subject of the first sentence. That line is followed by two more declarative sentences that also begin with "The joy-bringer," thus giving us the music of anaphora and drawing attention to the subject of the poem—gratitude.

This poem lists what we have to be grateful for. But Lux includes smaller lists within the poem, e.g., *skunk cabbage, ferns, a small brook*. While lots of poets use lists in their poems, Lux uses an unexpected numbered list. All these lists give us a feeling of abundance. The uneven line lengths also contribute to the feeling of abundance as they reach out and spill over.

As his speaker praises the joy-bringer, Lux uses a number of additional poetic techniques. Notice, for example, other uses of repetition. There's the repetition of words but as different parts of speech: *the joy-bringer brings*, and *a piano / falling on your head / and later at the hospital [you] fall in love*. There's also the simple repetition of *thanky, thanky*. Then notice line 5: *Gives the fish the river, and the river the fish*. This is a type of antithesis known as *antimetabole*, a rhetorical device in which the second half of a phrase or sentence reverses the word order of the first half.

Pay attention to Lux's use of diction. There is elegant phrasing as in *The Joy-Bringer / breaks the light through the oak leaves of dawn*. This is followed by a switch to biblical diction in *lets the cup runneth over*. Later, there's a switch to the colloquial language of *guess what* and *thanky, thanky*. Then Lux returns to elegant diction as he skillfully ends the poem with the image of *just-mown hay / cut an inch from its roots / to bleed its perfume into the air!*

Also pay attention to Lux's use of syntax. Notice how he follows the three opening declarative sentences with a complex sentence that begins with an *If* clause. The long clause ends with a colon and lurking after that is the subject and verb of the sentence: *the joy-bringer / arranged that*. Poets are often advised to avoid the colon and the exclamation point, but Lux uses two colons and three exclamation points. Such devices keep us on our toes and offer surprise.

Even with point of view Lux pulls a switch. Most of the poem addresses a general *you,* i.e., the recipient of joy, but at the end, the speaker switches to a direct address to the one who provides the joy: *Thank you, joy-bringer!*

Finally, notice how water runs as a common thread throughout the poem: *the river, the chilled artesian water,* and *a small brook.* The repetition of the image offers a subtle and interesting unifying device.

✎ ✎ ✎

For your own gratitude poem, first choose a name for your version of the joy-bringer. Then make a list of things for which you are grateful, some big, some small, e.g., salt, chocolate, flowers, morning. Try to find a common thread. For example, salt and chocolate are both food items. Exploit the thread, but subtly.

Write your first draft. Let your title run into your first line.

As you rework the draft, allow uneven line lengths as Lux does. Pay attention to your syntax. Pull a switch or two. Try your hand at antithesis or antimetabole. Break the rules of punctuation.

Also watch your diction. Mix it up a bit. Elegant and homely. Biblical and street.

Include some kind of special list. This might be a lettered list or a numbered one or even one with bullets.

Feeling cranky? Things not going your way? Then do just the opposite of a praise poem. Instead, do a curse or a complaint poem. Name the one responsible for all your woes. And employ the same strategies that Lux employs.

Sample Poems

The Queen of Despair

swirls a bit of helter-skelter into your morning coffee,
more charcoal than fresh cuppa.
The queen of despair at work:
Your chum's in prison for a reckless crime
she didn't commit—maximum security.
The planet is a pit and the pit is a planet.
The common thread here is the
stone in your chest,
the weighted limbs
so grounded—hell can't be much farther down.
The queen of despair
is throwing the first
pebble, metaphoric,
and you're lollygagging.
Fumigate the house with your slow burn,
your biceps like rocks.
Shower with juniper gel, comb your long wet hair.
Thank the queen of despair for turning you into
      a) a skipping stone,
      b) a stepping stone,
      c) a hot stone on someone's shoulder,
      d) a heavy-duty boulder.
Dance while you do the dishes.
Sing: *Sandman bring me a dream!*
Nowhere and anywhere
         is where
       you've
        got to get
          to.
Oh righteous queen of despair!
The oil of the earth is releasing
its smell.

—Lisa Young

The Rhythm-Giver

flips gold coin. Sun or moon.
The rhythm-giver rolls the ocean,
stakes shore. The rhythm-giver blows clouds,
taps rooftops and you lie down
beside green pastures, restored by songbirds.
Brings words to mouth and mouth to words.
If by a dime's rim you miss being hit by the ball
that shatters your window and a garlicked wind
leads to your neighbor's door,
you borrow a ladder. After, invited for dinner. Later,
a full course life. All the rhythm-giver's call.
Also, that time in the middle of 57th and Fifth,
traffic light changing, you stumble
when snap-fingers quick
a mid-air flip, you're an acrobatic dancer
holding a stranger's hand,
forfeiting pavement
after your five-mile hike
through bugs, sweat, and blister.
It's the rhythm-giver's play.
Hip-hooray for the rhythm-giver,
flipping upbeat with down.

—Denise Utt

Craft Tip #12: Make It and Break It

—Maggie Smith

The balance of mystery and clarity in a poem is always tricky. For me, a big part of revising is knowing when to say when. Sometimes the best thing I can do to improve a poem is to loosen my grip on it. It sounds a bit counterintuitive, but if you tie up every loose end, if you scrub all the strangeness and wildness out of it, you can revise the life right out of a poem. You can put its light out.

So if a poem feels stale or stiff to me, I'll sometimes shift it into prose to revise it. Why? We poets love the line. We love to make them and break them. How many of us, working on a prose poem, are tempted back to lineation? I, for one, feel like I'm writing with one hand tied behind my back without lines; a whole set of possibilities is out of my reach.

On the other hand, though—the hand I can still use—I have every other element at my disposal: metaphor, image, syntax, diction, assonance, consonance, alliteration, internal rhyme, rhythm, repetition, and so on. Because I am acutely aware of my inability to rely on line breaks for double meanings, emphasis, and pacing, I tend to shift more weight onto these other aspects of the poem.

Recasting a poem in prose takes my focus off the lines as such and helps me focus on the music in the poem, and on syntactical variety: statements versus questions, fragments versus grammatically complete sentences. It also often helps me loosen up the diction. I've had some major breakthroughs with poems by taking line breaks off the table.

I suggest giving it a try. When you're satisfied with the poem in its temporary prose form, return to lineation. Now you can turn your attention to line length and how you want the poem to move. We each have our own tics and preferences in our poems: default line lengths, stanzas, even types of sentences. On the bright side, these aspects of craft make our poems recognizably ours. They're how we can instantly distinguish a Louise Glück poem from a Mei-mei Berssenbrugge poem from a Matthew Zapruder poem. But we should continue to question these choices, too, and make sure they serve the poem at hand.

When you return to lineation, consider James Longenbach's types of lines: *end-stopped* (lines which end with punctuation), *annotated* (lines in which enjambments *annotate* the syntax of the poem, emphasizing parts of the sentence that would not be emphasized otherwise), and *parsed* (lines in which the sentences break across lines at predictable points, according to natural divisions in the syntax). I think of parsed lines as being broken with the grain of the sentence, while annotated lines— what we might call heavily enjambed lines—cut against the grain.

Each kind of line comes with caveats. When you return to lines in your draft, use a variety to propel the poem and to enact meaning. Annotating lines can feel too self-conscious or gimmicky. Parsing lines can feel too expected. In a poem with primarily end-stopped and parsed lines, occasional radical enjambments could be used for emphasis and to enact a shift in thinking or action within the poem. In a heavily enjambed poem, end-stopped lines will put the brakes on and draw attention to those moments. The same applies to syntax, when short sentences or fragments may be interspersed with long, complex sentences. Remember: it's not only the line that breaks; it's the expectation that's set and then broken.

Poem and Prompt

Epithalamion for the Long Dead

Once there was a girl
with a trunk full
of lace and beeswax

given to a man
with forty acres, a rough
beamed house on a hill.

She perfected the art
of biscuits, cooked her hens'
suns in cast iron.

How warm it always was,
and in the quiet night,
she waited

for him to slowly pull
the ribbons of her bodice,
to take the moon in his hand.

Now theirs is one of those
homesteads seen from the highway,
disappeared

to just a set of flagstone stairs
in a field, leading nowhere.

In what were rooms, yarrow
and snake grass. The barn
choked with kudzu.

But there is something
in the way a dragonfly wants
a pane to tap its wings against.

Her blackberries still grow
along the thorny fence,
giving their blossoms to bees.

They have a thousand
grandchildren who will never
find their way home.

To them they are just names
and dates on the first page
of a cracked-spine Bible.

—Danielle Sellers

An epithalamion is a wedding song or poem in honor of a bride
and bridegroom. There is a long tradition of such poems, but
usually they are written for a living couple at the beginning of a
marriage. Sellers breaks with tradition by writing for a long-
dead couple. Her ironic title heralds that breach.

The poem begins in the manner of a fairy tale's *Once upon a
time*. We are introduced to a girl with a small dowry and to a
man with forty acres on a hill. We are then given the merest
details of their lives together and taken into the future, long after
their deaths.

The poem is told from third person point of view, but we are
very aware of a storyteller. The poem contains many elements
of a narrative poem: the storyteller, characters (but without
names), setting (but we don't know where exactly), chronology
(but no dates), conclusion. However, what makes this poem
special is the fusion between narrative and lyric.

Notice, for example, the lyric elements of imagery and figurative
language. How sensual were the nights when the wife *waited //
for him to slowly pull / the ribbons of her bodice, / to take the
moon in his hand*. The metaphor's *moon* is surely a stand-in for
the wife's breast and a nice match to the *hens' // suns* she
cooked. Then there's a lovely image used to express the idea

that what the bride began continues on long after her death: *Her blackberries still grow / along the thorny fence, / giving their blossoms to bees*. The alliteration of that stanza is hard to ignore—*blackberries, blossoms, bees*.

Synecdoche is effectively used to reveal all that has been lost. What was once their home is now reduced to *just a set of flagstone stairs / in a field, leading nowhere*. Notice, too, how the hyperbole of *a thousand / grandchildren* emphasizes the couple's reach into the future.

✐ ✐ ✐

Let's try an epithalamion. First, choose a couple, maybe your grandparents or great grandparents, maybe a couple whose wedding you attended, maybe a couple you invent. Perhaps you and your spouse. Sketch in the details of their married life. Where did they live? What were their daily lives like? Did they have children? Imagine far into the future, long after their deaths. What evidence is there that once they lived?

Use third person point of view as you narrate the story. Leave out the specifics; instead, generalize, e.g., if the couple lived in Ohio, make it the Midwest. No names, no dates.

One of the challenges of this assignment is to fuse together narrative and lyric. Include some imagery as you tell the story. Bring in other lyric elements such as metaphor, synecdoche, and hyperbole.

Pay attention to your language. Keep it simple. Work in some alliteration, scattering it throughout your poem.

Alternate end-stopped and enjambed stanzas.

Sample Poems

Epithalamion for That Couple,
They Looked So Happy

Once there was a young man
with a shadow space
where his leg should have been,

who married a girl
who could have been a pinup,
the next Betty Grable,

all curved calves
and delicate ankles,
all waltz and sway.

How well it started:
linked elbows,
feeding each other wedding cake,

guest book overflowing.
At night she studied
the map of his body

with its fallen-away continent,
learned to love
what was absent.

Now theirs is one of those mysteries
seen from down the years,
how something worked its way

between them
like some island that rises
from the sea

to redraw the maps
and tide charts, something
to run ships aground.

How they rode separate rivers
down from the Continental
Divide.

But there is something
in the way a daughter
wears her mother's rings,

hangs her father's dress blues
in a black bag
at the back of her closet.

Their house still stands
on the suburban street
where the daughter learned to ride a bike.

The roses they planted
still drop their petals
beneath the kitchen window.

They have a tight clutch
of grandchildren who will never
know their voices

but who speak their language
all the same, who spend their time
drawing maps and charting other continents.

—Jennifer Saunders

Making Butter

Without lipstick, lace or jewels,
she was mellow of skin with cast-iron bones.

He was overalls cranky, building the house
they would live in, and later would talk all day

to his cows, chickens, and garden.
If it rained, he read his tented newspaper

at the table, waiting for dinner.
Morning but a sliver, he was milking a cow,

pinging a tin pail. She skimmed off cream
that had risen to milk's top and,

with wooden bowl and spoon, churned
until the cream turned to butter. She waited

in housedress for him at night to spoon her
from corset, and spread with rising flesh.

Now they're spread somewhere in the lacey night garden.
Hardly their house anymore, without cow or chickens,

just strangers who lounge, sip cocktails,
and dip crackers in hummus.

Their children in cities now,
churn revolving doors for their butter.

—Denise Utt

Top Tips: Ten Tips for Poets: A Prose Poem

—Dorianne Laux

One must eat and sleep well. You need all your strength for poems. One needs **two** read lots of poems. Memorize at least **three** poems you love. Tear **four** good poems apart, dissect them to find out how they work. Imitate **five** good poems. Keep an image notebook. Write down **six** images a day. No commentary, just images. Cull once every **seven** months for poems. Go to the beach, or a lake, or a river, any body of water will do, stare into the bird bath, get one of those little solar plates with a spout and watch the birds bathe. Go down to the train tracks, or the depot, or sit at a bus stop, a Laundromat, watch and listen, take in the smells, the textures, the sounds, write it down or don't write it down, just get out of the damn house for a minimum of **eight** minutes. Make friends with musicians, artists, sculptors, composers, dancers, go to museums and outdoor events, visit anything abandoned or unmaintained. Sit in the waiting room of a hospital, the DMV, an upscale restaurant, say you're waiting for **nine** friends. When you get mad, count to **ten**, then write a poem.

Bonus Prompt: The One Sense Poem

Select a single sense, but not sight. Choose from taste, smell, sound, touch, or motion.

Now select a distinct setting, e.g., the circus, the beach or boardwalk, the gym, a police station, the zoo, a bird sanctuary, or an arboretum.

With your setting in mind, make a list of images that rely on the sense you chose.

Use that material in a poem.

As you revise, select your two strongest lines. Use one of them as the opening line, the other as the closing line.

Now make the rest of the lines just as strong as the opening and closing lines. This might necessitate reordering lines.

V. Crafting Surprise

Poetry is an act of mischief.

—Theodore Roethke

Craft Tip #13: Using the Line to Surprise

—Meg Day

As a young reader, the poetry I pursued was steeped in data; I savored the care and attention with which a poet would labor to make vivid with detail a fact that I did not already understand or an event I could not have experienced. Perhaps I, like many of my students, was easy to please in that regard. When one is still at the forefront of a lifetime of realization and information gathering, fresh exposure and insight are transformative, but not hard to come by. The more I read, however, the more the pleasure torqued; I sought, instead, epiphany.

It's a familiar story to those who study creative writing. We are taught that poets see differently, better. I read to experience the surprise of finding something common made freshly strange (or strangely fresh?) by its delivery on the page, and then read again to try to learn how to *ostranenie*—to defamiliarize. Indeed, metaphor is often the first trope we learn to associate with poetry. *They're new eyes*, a graduate professor once said when I asked if she liked the book of poems she was reading, *and I can't yet quite see.*

While I won't argue for or against the idea that a poem should reveal something truly or only recently foreign, I will argue on behalf of surprise. A poem's potential for linguistic surprise is buried in its image, its sound, and its lineation. Surprise on the level of the line interests me most because it has such a capacity for multiplicity and can tap so easily into each of those aforementioned poetic obsessions: new information, new perspective, *new eyes.*

Or, really, *new brain.* Of what is a line capable? When a poet breaks a line in the middle of a sentence, the enjambment requires action: move to the next line to complete the sentence's semantic message. These breaks often play a large part in moving the reader down the page, as in a narrative fashion. True, sometimes enjambment can speed up a poem or slow it down, but I typically give credit to the length and consistency of the line and its meter when it comes to pacing. But what if we expected more of our lines than simply shuttling, however beautifully, the reader from one place to the next? What if we demanded of our lines the experiential novelty some have come to insist upon in a poem's subject matter?

While many of us were taught to break a line according to meter or where our breath indicated a pause, I think most of us come to our understanding of a line's real potential via wordplay and puns. Long before we're thinking of enjambment, we're learning to keep up with double entendre and innuendo, often nefarious, so as to always be on the inside of a joke in the schoolyard, to be one step ahead.

Like double meaning, a good line break is slippery. It uses wit to exploit ambiguity in a which-way-are-you-moving two-step dance that anticipates a reader's next intellectual move and disrupts it by allowing meaning to multiply by straddling the line's end. The reader experiences a new kind of mental defamiliarization when this happens, not unlike the thrill of a sleight of hand. Like a good joke, however, a solid line break doesn't leave its reader more than a beat behind; without a quick followup—or appreciative pause to revel—a line that doesn't land evokes the same response as a failed joke: awkward silence, future avoidance.

How do we up the ante on lineation? We ask our lines to do and be more by putting them always already in conversation with the line that comes prior to and the line that follows. I call a good line break *industrious* because it does the heavy lifting of a) building off of the semantic meaning in the line that precedes it, b) satisfying the semantic needs of the line on which it breaks, c) providing enough tension—by way of suspending that semantic need—to propel additional meaning into the line that follows, and d) preventing the reader, by way of surprise, from moving too swiftly down the page.

Poet Kimberly Johnson's work regularly employs industrious lines. In "Blanks" Johnson takes every opportunity to outthink and then reward her reader on the level of the line:

The sun rolls up like jackpot,
the thousand blinding coins of it spilling
across my windshield's dustdapple.
Glory be: my lucky day, flush and prime
as a fresh dime, as if the world been spit-shined.
The asphalt ahead's gleamed to a high glare
and I play my pedal past the red line, and faster.
Must be what faith feels like, to drive believing
in the persistence of highway lines
whose white paint's whitened to a wide white field,
to glimpse in swift periphery and guess
you've passed a rest-stop's spare oasis,
to catch the flicker of a cactus shadow
as a signpost toward some providential end.
If on such a visionary road
I should see the world's material scroll
back to show whatever lies behind
who would blame me? Who'd blame if I sublimed
each raw thing into a revelation—
the big-rig flipping its rockchip stigmata,
the naugahyde peeling an unction
from my thigh. But no. Faith's for the sucker
whose luck's run out. Faith is for the fear
that sometimes you get cherries, and sometimes
you pull the handle and it comes up blanks.

A good line sits on the edge of implosion, simultaneously expanding and contracting in semantic meaning. A good line develops tension that is contrapuntal; it resists the pull of gravity down the vertical thrust of the poem by rewarding the reader for pausing at the end of each semantic unit.

Johnson places each line as a building block in a larger construction that reveals itself to the reader slowly: *Must be what faith feels like, to drive believing / in the persistence of highway lines / whose white paint's whitened to a wide white field*. To sidestep expectation in this way draws special attention to the poem and to the images and the sounds the poet is engaging on behalf of the narrative. With each enjambment, Johnson opens possibility horizontally—*I should see the world's material scroll*—but then narrows possibility vertically—*back to show whatever lies behind*—before repurposing *scroll* as a verb.

When it comes to tightening my line breaks, I start by taking the advice I give my students: be intentional. Actively choosing where to break a line can greatly improve the dynamism of a poem on the level of structure. Other good habits I've adopted include using unusual meter or the ghost of inherited form to help reimagine what might be possible for the lines of a poem draft. Sometimes, I experiment with removing all the line breaks and look instead for interesting word pairings or wordplay already present in the poem; anyone can train themselves to notice these sites of potential and play with how best to use them. I can then choose to rewrite the poem around a particularly industrious line break. Often, this reveals a new axis on which the poem can spin, or spin off, creating surprise as much in the poet as in the reader.

Poem and Prompt

Driving the Beast

In the thick brush
they spend the hottest part of the day,
        soaking their hooves
in the trickle of mountain water
        the ravine hoards
on behalf of the oleander.
        You slung your gun
across your back in order to heave
        a huge grey stone
over the edge, so it rolled, then leaped
        and crashed below.
This is what it took to break the shade,
        to drive the beast,
not to mention a thrumming of wings
        into the sky,
a wild confetti of frantic grouse,
        but we had slugs,
not shot, and weren't after their small meat,
        but the huge ram's,
whose rack you'd seen last spring, and whose stench
        now parted air,
that scat-caked, rut-ripe perfume of beast.
        Watch now, he runs,
you said, launching another boulder,
        then out it sprang
through a gap in some pine, brown and black
        with spiraled horns
impossibly agile for its size.
        But, yes, he fell
with one shot, already an idea
        of meat for fire
by the time we'd scrambled through the scree.
        And that was all.
No, you were careful, even tender,

          with the knife-work,
slitting the body wide with one stroke
          then with your hands
lifting entire the miraculous
          liver and heart,
emptying the beast on the mountain.
          Later, it rained,
knocking dust off the patio stones.
          Small frogs returned
from abroad to sing in the stream beds.
          We sat and drank.
The beast talked to its rope in the tree.
          And then you spoke:
no more, you said, *enough with mourning,*
          then rose to turn
our guts, already searing on the fire.

                    —Christopher Bakken

Bakken describes his poem as in conversation with another poem: Robert Frost's "The Most of It." Look closely and you'll see some similarities between the two.

Frost's poem captures an unexpected event in nature as does Bakken's. Frost's is written in iambic pentameter; Bakken's is not, but it does rely a lot on iambic feet. Frost's poem ends with the phrase *and that was all*. Bakken incorporates those exact words into his poem.

Let's now look more closely at Bakken's poem.

Even before reading the poem, we notice its pattern of indentations. Bakken begins with an indented line, then repeats the indentation every other line. He employs a syllabic pattern of 4/9. Each indented line has 4 syllables. Each longer line has 9. This syllable count determines where the line breaks occur. The visual pattern is reflected in the rhythm when the poem is read aloud. Notice, too, that the indented lines, with only a few exceptions, consist of monosyllabic words—the same as Frost's closing phrase.

The speaker speaks from the distance of time. The result of using past tense is a quiet, retrospective tone. Bakken also employs a direct address to an auditor, a *you*, the speaker's companion in the scene. This adds a touch of intimacy to the poem. We are listening to a private conversation.

The poem is rife with descriptive details—of the setting, the ram, and the gutting of the beast. Notice especially the sensory details: *the trickle of mountain water*, the *huge grey stone* crashing, *a thrumming of wings, a wild confetti of frantic grouse,* the *stench* of the beast, *that scat-caked, rut-ripe perfume of beast, slitting the body wide with one stroke,* the frogs singing in the *stream beds.* We hear, we see, we smell.

As you read the poem aloud, notice the consonance, particularly the predominance of hard *k* sounds: e.g., *thick, soaking, back, crashed, break, sky, rack, black.* The repeated sound scattered throughout gives the poem a fierceness and a rhythm.

Some readers might feel that an attribution is necessary, but with a poem as famous as Frost's, it's likely that Bakken assumes his readers will recognize the debt to Frost without being told.

✎ ✎ ✎

For your own conversation poem, first select a poem that's made an impact on you. Read it carefully and repeatedly. Then recall or contrive a situation similar to but distinct from the one in the poem. That situation will be the subject of your poem. Borrow a line or phrase from the model poem.

Now quickly write a first draft and incorporate the borrowed words.

Let's work with syllabics and visual pattern. Read through your draft. Can you perceive any kind of pattern or rhythm, perhaps one suggested by the borrowed words? Zero in on a pattern for your own poem. It could be 4/9 but doesn't have to be. It could be 5/10 or 6/8 or whatever you decide. As you continue to revise, imitate the pattern of indentations, indenting every other line or perhaps every three or four lines.

Now consider the sounds in your poem. Zero in on a single consonant and exploit it throughout the poem as you revise. You might choose a hard sound or a soft one, depending on the subject of your poem. Also, try to work with monosyllables. Achieving both the consonance and the monosyllabic emphasis may necessitate changing some diction. That's a good thing.

Use past tense. Make the poem reflective. Bring in an auditor, a *you* to whom you address your words, someone who was perhaps a participant but not necessarily in the situation described in the poem.

Pay attention to your descriptive details. Be generous with them and try to hit several senses—sight, sound, taste, smell, touch, motion.

Decide whether or not to include an attribution.

Sample Poems

Letter

> *Whatever you think, I have scarcely*
> *thought of you.*
> —"Letter to____," Mary Oliver

I have scarcely thought of you
  for six weeks, since

you vanished the way a cat
  slips out a door,

silently. I admit life
  was as empty

as your closet.I was like
  a bird flying back

to my old woods, my old perch:
  I soon took up

my old life: swimming, hiking,
  reading, writing.

I'm repairing the garden:
  after you left

the flowers mourned, expressing
  their grief like girls

when their favorite teacher
  suddenly quits.

My two-year-old peonies
  threw their fistfuls

of petals to the ground, like
   toddlers throwing

tantrums. Everyone hung
   their heads—even

those spoiled divas, the dahlias.
   I could not coax

a better posture from them.
   What should I do?

Maybe take a cruise to Greece,
   wandering through

toppled ruins, embraced by vines?
   Or volunteer

to train guide dogs, as I once
   did? Whatever

I do, I won't think of you
   as I drink wine

in a Sonoma vineyard,
   champagne winking

at me like the waitresses.
   I'll never long

for your arms again. I swear
   you don't exist,

though you once hugged me the way
   a starfish clings

to a piling, refusing
   to let go. What

could pry you away? I asked.
   "Nothing," you said.

"Not even rip tides." It's true,
   it turns out, love's

as perishable as plums,
   grapes, nuts, goat's milk.

I will probably be in Rome
   or Bologna

should you, for a split second,
   think of me. Still,

though I scarcely think of you,
   don't be surprised

if I pick up your phone call.
   It's just habit.

                —Bob Bradshaw

When I Was One and Twenty

after A. E. Housman

When I was twenty-one and thought I knew
      many things
about marriage and muffins and babies
      and sleeping
through unwanted kisses, babies' murmurs,
      the full moon
burning through cheap, ugly maroon curtains,
      not one word
anyone told me might have rescued me
      from myself.

At thirty-one I believed I'd mastered
      being smart.
But no, I was still so dumb, mixed-up, so
      unprepared,
standing in front of my college students
      pretending
to know something about anything.
      Minor farce:
my two bad marriages, my stud boyfriend
      who couldn't.

Now I have muddled past seventy-one,
      babies grown,
mortgage paid off, books made, merry wrinkles,
      and I know
it's true, it's true, that I don't know much:
      minor truths
about wishes and messes, the magic
      of watching
hummingbirds, kids, clouds, how they rush toward
      tomorrow.

—Penelope Scambly Schott

Craft Tip #14: Truth's Surprise

—Lawrence Raab

One of the most famous and most useful pieces of writerly advice is Emily Dickinson's *Tell all the Truth but tell it slant*— But what exactly does she mean by this? And how can it be helpful, either to the writer or the reader?

As a wise assertion, that sentence seems to stand on its own. But Dickinson's words aren't a remark; they're the first line of a poem (#1129), and before we think more about what they mean, we should see where they belong:

> Tell all the Truth but tell it slant—
> Success in Circuit lies
> Too bright for our infirm Delight
> The Truth's superb surprise
>
> As lightning to the children eased
> With explanation kind
> The Truth must dazzle gradually
> Or every man be blind—

Slant, the OED reports, means *a course or movement in an oblique direction*, although another definition given is *a sly hint or sarcasm*. That *sly hint* reminds me of Robert Frost's claim that poets like to speak *in parables and in hints and in indirections*. For the reader, the poet's use of indirection produces the surprise of discovery, which can become the revelation of truth.

One of Frost's strategies, however, is to pretend to assert the truth directly. *Something there is that doesn't love a wall* is a wisdom statement repeated twice in his poem "Mending Wall." Yet what doesn't love a wall is offset by what apparently does: *Good fences make good neighbors.* This the poem also repeats twice.

Which is true? Many unwary readers find themselves lining up on the side they take to be the poet's. What he wants—what the poem endorses—is the tearing down of everything that separates us. But this, I believe, is a trap, a way of ignoring what is *slant* in the poem, the discovery of which might lead to a different and more substantial kind of thinking. After all, *Good fences make good neighbors* is not clearly an endorsement of building walls and erecting barriers, since mending fences is a neighborly act that joins rather than separates.

Neither of Frost's doubled statements represents the truth of the poem, and so we must resist turning that wall into an inflexible symbol. We must pause and wonder why the speaker, who is not Frost *exactly*, is the one who initiates the repair of the wall, even as he seems to argue against its necessity. We need to be attentive to the speaker's desire to be playful (*Spring is the mischief in me, and I wonder / If I could put a notion in his head*), and then worry about why his attitude toward his neighbor becomes suddenly harsh at the end (*I see him there… like an old-stone savage armed*).

We might recognize, as the poem's apparently contradictory statements play off each other, that we are meant to think twice about choosing up sides. The course of arriving at this understanding is one way of describing what the poem *means*. All of its sly hints lead us away from an attitude that merely confirms what we thought we knew already. What we want (to quote from Frost's "The Figure a Poem Makes") is *a revelation, or a series of revelations, as much for the poet as for the reader*.

Of particular interest to me here is how the poet's experience in making the poem may be duplicated for the reader. Poets who begin writing with a preconceived idea of what their poems will mean are likely to end up only with that preconceived idea. They deprive themselves of those truths that might appear unexpectedly through the act of composition. Not knowing, at least at first, is essential to discovery. We surprise ourselves into understanding. *It is but a trick poem*, writes Frost, *and no poem at all if the best of it was thought of first and saved for the last. It finds its own name as it goes and discovers the best waiting for it in some final phrase at once wise and sad.*

This is Dickinson's *Success in Circuit*. And yet a circuit, to return to the OED, is not only *a round-about journey* but also

134

the course traversed by an electrical current between the two poles of a battery. In this double sense the circuitous path can also be, paradoxically, the most direct, a bright leap from pole to pole, a dazzling jolt of light that seems suddenly to reveal what the poem has gradually come to understand.

Poem and Prompt

Still Life with Long-Range View

To return to the cabin you rented one long and happy weekend
    two years earlier is, of course, to find it diminished—
not in the way going back to some childhood landmark
    will shrink it to life-size, but an actual lessening:
the wooden bear you posed beside for photographs
    replaced by a smaller bear. Empty hooks where the hammock hung.

The fountain's still basin is clouded with larvae and home
    to three skittery frogs. Only the trees sloping
down the hill are greater now, their tops beginning to block
    the mountain view. And in the bushes by the porch,
something vast and moving, shifting against the leaves.

To return to a house you so briefly inhabited
    is to acknowledge your own diminishing. How could
you think it would be waiting, unchanged, for you alone?
    Try the view from every window, then try to tell yourself
the mountains in the distance will always be visible
    over the trees. That the creature in the undergrowth
is some small thing, casting a long shadow of sound.

—Chelsea Rathburn

Rathburn chooses a topic that will probably ring a familiar note for many readers. Someone returns to a place she'd visited in the past and finds it changed. Most of us find that our revisited place *seems* smaller and different, but this person's place is literally diminished, e.g., a large wooden bear has been replaced by a smaller one. Following several such examples, the speaker gives us one exception, i.e., something that is now bigger—the trees.

Notice that the poet uses second person point of view. This puts the speaker outside of the experience, as if it's one she witnessed someone else experiencing. Consider the effect this has on the tone of the poem. Does it make it warmer or colder, closer or more distant?

Notice also the form of the poem. Rathburn uses infinitives to help structure the poem and create a rhythm. Then the indentations that occur every other line give the poem an elegant appearance, but, more importantly, they parallel the back and forth motion of the poem, between then and now, between what was and what is.

Notice the turn that occurs at the midway point. The sudden appearance of *something vast and moving, shifting against the leaves* adds a note of danger to the poem. Whatever this is is revisited at the end of the poem where we learn that there is a *creature in the undergrowth* and that it's *casting a long shadow of sound.*

Consider that *long shadow of sound.* What an interesting use of *synesthesia*, i.e., a mixture of two senses, here sight and sound. What does this figure add to the poem?

Note the question in stanza 3. That question seems to chastise the *you* for her arrogance in thinking that things would remain the same just for her.

✐ ✐ ✐

Choose a house or other physical structure that you returned to after an absence. Perhaps a house or apartment you lived in or one you visited for a period of time. How did the place seem changed when you returned? Brainstorm a list of changes. Include one opposite kind of change, e.g., if your place seems smaller, include something that appears bigger; if your place seems darker, include something that appears lighter; if your place seems dirtier, include something that appears cleaner. Feel free to invent the details and feel free to increase the number of years beyond the two that Rathburn uses.

Using second person point of view, begin your draft, incorporating the changes and details.

At the midway point, insert an ominous image, some kind of turn in the poem. Return to this image at the end of your poem.

Insert a question in which the speaker addresses the *you*. If it works, keep it. If not, feel free to delete it.

Can you use synesthesia?

Find a form that reflects your subject matter.

Sample Poems

Finding the House on Trimble Street

The house, once white and raw, has matured into gold. Ripened maples in October red temptingly frame the remembrance. The garage neatly unfolds from the side, the lawn edged in definition. You imagine responsible owners, their unblemished lives. They don't know who stacked cement blocks into a basement bunker. A girl slept above the so-called shelter, and when the sirens roared, her parents brought her downstairs into the dank cave. Sometimes it was a tornado with its green sky, and sometimes it was a bomb with its puff of smoke and a white rabbit in the magician's hat. When she played outside in the woods behind the house, she watched the color of the sky for changes—pink, purple, chartreuse. In the grass, she looked for a four-leaf clover, but never found it. She crouched to examine helpless red worms on the sidewalk in front, searching for a nightcrawler or a bloodworm that bites. At night she lay awake for hours in her small bed, listening for the plinky-plink on the roof. Or the solitary train whistle from the nearby tracks.

> freight train passes by
> taking time and distance
> leaving memories

—Luanne Castle

Return

But you *lived* here. You brought the baby home here,
    driving as if on eggs in the old yellow Plymouth
up the curving half-mile drive planted with daffodils,
    past the front lake with its Canada geese, past
the Angus bull in his field and the Angus cows in theirs,
    past the low white house and the swimming pool
nestled behind a squared-off boxwood hedge
    where, in summers, your kids were welcome to swim
from ten to noon (*chop chop, out by lunchtime!*
    your landlady, the famous beauty, would tell them)—
you brought the baby home to this tiny rented cottage
    on the vast estate south of Charlottesville, with its
three barns, its fields, the steep hill down to Ray's,
    the farm manager's house, where his hound dog
flopped in the sun, and beyond Ray's into the forest.
    Your kids picked forget-me-nots down by the stream
that ran through the woods, and rambled around
    to find stuff for "The Nature Table"—lichen-furred
sticks, flaps of moss, a turtle shell, striate rocks,
    and once, lambs' tails, yes, actual curling lambs' tails,
that had fallen off when Ray cut the circulation
    with rubber bands. Did you think it would not change?
Did you think the enormous king snake would still
    twine itself in August through the pool's boxwood,
and the cows would still bellow for their babies,
    and the children would still—Ah, there was sorrow
even then, fights sometimes, and because all but the baby
    were children of divorce, wracking sobs at partings.
Did you think you could remember without pain?
    But there was so much love. And to go back
after nearly thirty years, and to see the fields empty,
    geese gone, cows gone, sheep gone, peeling paint

and broken windows on the big house, pool a stink
      of algae, flagstone terraces choked with weeds,
and your own little cottage derelict, capsized, moldy—
      you peered through a grimy window and what
did you see? A plastic doll, some trash, a box.
      Nothing, nothing. Not even the ghosts of children.

—Ann Fisher-Wirth

Craft Tip #15: Throwing the Reins upon the Horse's Neck

—Chris Forhan

The poems I love best have something secret adrift in them—an *it* they can't reveal completely because this *it* is beyond words. We can coax such secrets into our poems, into the dim light at the periphery of our language, by letting that language go where it wants to, beyond our conscious intentions. We must cede some control to chance, to the deep designs lurking within syntax and the psyche, to dumb luck.

If a poem seems to be too much the product of the rational, evaluating, judging mind—and is thus composed with a surfeit of discursive rhetoric or merely dazzling, witty tricks of language—it can seem pushy or simplistic, too knowing and not knowing enough. As I heard Heather McHugh say in a lecture once, a good poem has within it *something that overwhelms its own intellect*.

In his essay "The Poet," Emerson says something similar; he speaks of a power *beyond the energy of [our] possessed and conscious intellect* that we experience *by abandonment to the nature of things*. He reminds us that as *the traveller who has lost his way, throws his reins on his horse's neck, and trusts to the instinct of the animal to find his road, so must we do with the divine animal who carries us through the world*.

How, in our poems, can we partake of an energy beyond the *conscious intellect*? How can we let our *divine animal* lead the way? Dean Young proposes one strategy: When accidents happen, don't correct them; follow them. *Always turn in the direction of the skid*, he writes. That advice comes from a poem, "How I Get My Ideas," which is structured mainly as a list of tips for writers, one of the last of which is to give yourself entirely over to the unconscious by sleeping. After offering that instruction, Young's poem surprises itself—as a sleeper is surprised by his dreams—with the appearance of an unexpected character:

you'll just have to wait which
may involve sleeping which may involve
dreaming and sometimes dreaming works.
Father, why have you returned,
dirt on your morning vest?

When that father appears—not as the consequence of a logical sequence of thoughts but as a sudden vision, a gift, an upending of our understanding that the dead stay dead—the poem goes deeper than we, and perhaps it, expected, into memory and grief, into the worlds of Hamlet and Orpheus and Gilgamesh, teeming with psychic and emotional material.

If we find ourselves surprised by something we have written, if it seems to have come from nowhere and has little to do with what has otherwise been on our mind, if it seems as though it probably belongs in a different poem, we may be wise to follow it. It may beckon us toward a rich and murky realm: a more interesting place than the mental real estate the poem has heretofore been inhabiting.

I don't know the circumstances of the writing of the following poem by Franz Wright, but I do know that it is filled with veerings, unexpected turns that make the poem travel indirectly but relentlessly toward a destination I would not have anticipated:

Cloudless Snowfall

Great big flakes like white ashes
at nightfall descending
abruptly everywhere
and vanishing
in this hand like the host
on somebody's put-out tongue, she
turns the crucifix over
to me, still warm
from her touch two years later
and thank you,
I say all alone—
Vast *whisp-whisp* of wingbeats
awakens me and I look up

at a minute-long string of black geese
following low past the moon the white
course of the snow-covered river and
by the way thank You for
keeping Your face hidden, I
can hardly bear the beauty of this world.

I am interested in this poem's rapid shifts of thought and perception. The snow seems at first to be vanishing *everywhere*, but then, no, it is *vanishing / in this hand*. The poem has zoomed in dizzyingly from a wide shot—of *everywhere*—to a close-up of a single human hand. Then, through a surprising simile, the snow melting on the hand is compared with the Communion host melting on the believer's *put-out tongue*. Already we are far from where we began. Then an unnamed *she* enters the poem, her appearance feeling all the more sudden for the strange syntax employed in that moment. The poem's first six lines can be read as an elaborately extended noun phrase that is awaiting its predicate, but that phrase turns out to be a fragment—one that is abandoned suddenly, as in a jump cut, with the comma before *she*.

The poem has become about this woman and about religious contemplation. She *turns the crucifix over*, and the line break after the preposition allows us, for a moment, to presume that she is revealing the back side of the crucifix, but then, no, we discover that the phrase *turns the crucifix over* means to hand over; she is giving the speaker the crucifix, which is *still warm*. That makes sense; the heat of the woman's hand is still felt on the crucifix the moment after it leaves her grasp. But then, no, it turns out that the warmth (understood now to be metaphorical) remains two years after the gift was offered. The speaker says *thank you*—to the woman, we might presume. But that's not it exactly; the next line announces that he is speaking while *all alone*. What is going on here?

Two lines later, he wakes up. Ah, it was a dream! Now the immediate, physical world, embodied by those geese and the moon and the river, takes over the poem and takes over the speaker's field of vision until he surprises us, and seemingly himself, with a thought: *by the way thank You*, he says, and the poem becomes suddenly an address to God. It becomes an expression of awe. The speaker *can hardly bear the beauty of this world*. The poem has careened rapidly down the page and around multiple corners of consciousness, with each veering moving the speaker inexorably toward this climactic experience of astonishment and near-wordlessness, which is underscored by the restrained, perfect iambic pentameter of the final line.

I have no idea whether Wright himself, in the initial stages of composing this poem, knew where it was going. It sure sounds, though, as if he didn't, and "Cloudless Snowfall" is better for it; the poem, in giving itself over to its impulses, becomes an act of revelation, for the speaker and for us.

I was once trying to write a poem that was filled with waves and sailors and sloops and coves, and it wasn't working. The poem wasn't going anywhere in particular, maybe because it wasn't *coming* from anywhere in particular. Then, reading Apollinaire, I chanced upon this line: *Flame flame I do what you desire.* Something in me knew that that voice, a hauntingly incantatory direct address to the inhuman and elemental, needed to enter my poem. I wrote, *Water, whatever you want, I want to want that*, and then I followed that voice, ignorant of where it might lead. I threw my reins upon the horse's neck.

I finished the poem, and, years later, it is one of the rare poems of mine for which I continue to feel a fondness. It still seems invigorated by something ineffable, some meaningful mystery, because I allowed myself to relax into a state of unknowing; I let that horse take charge.

Poem and Prompt

Emerson Street

This is the exact spot
on Emerson Street,
where August Dolan kicked me

so spectacularly in the balls,
that I dropped to my knees, whispered *Oh*
and coughed out a baby blackbird—

the aftermath of my innocence,
that flew off and took its place
in the sycamores with the other crows

gathered to witness my revenge.
Dolan twisted out of his coat,
but I grabbed his tie,

garroting him one-handed,
sizing up his reddening face with my free fist.
Even now I feel with pleasure his fat

cheek blacken on my knuckles.
Sister Aloysius Gonzaga,
Sacred Heart's simian principal—

she favored Zira,
the hazel-eyed chimpanzee
animal psychologist, played by Kim

Hunter in *Planet of the Apes*—
witnessed the entire affair
from her office, hauled us in,

backhanded Augie so hard,
his scorched face peeled by lunch,
knocked us both into the marble stairwell

with a titanium yardstick,
then whaled the Communion
of Saints out of us as we lay there—

prompting the life-size statue
of Our Lady of Perpetual Help
to jitter on her plinth,

though she winked
when I gazed up at her in my stupor.
Birds have testicles,

but keep them hidden,
out of harm's way,
inside their bodies.

—Joseph Bathanti

Bathanti's poem is an excellent example of a narrative poem that works. It has the elements of narrative: characters, place, conflict, resolution. But it works so well because it's more than just a story. It's a story told lyrically.

The poet wastes no time getting to the main action: a childhood fight in the schoolyard. Then the poem turns fanciful as the youthful speaker, after being kicked hard in his most tender place, opens his mouth and out flies a baby blackbird. The now-mature speaker interprets this as a loss of innocence symbol. How interesting, though, that Bathanti turns his symbol into a witness to the action that follows, i.e., the boy's revenge as he beats the tar out of his attacker.

Notice the poetic techniques that add lyricism to the poem. We find lots of alliteration, e.g., in the *f* sounds in *his reddening face with my free fist. / Even now I feel with pleasure his fat...*

And then there's consonance, e.g., in the *k* sounds in *cheek blacken on my knuckles.*

We also find some notable figures of speech. There's an allusion to a movie, *The Planet of the Apes*, as the nun who imposes discipline is compared to one of the characters in the film. We also find hyperbole as the narrator *backhanded Augie so hard, / his scorched face peeled by lunch.* And the nun *whaled the Communion / of Saints out of us as we lay there.* Personification comes in as the statue of Our Lady of Perpetual Help winks at the narrator.

Finally, the poet uses a circular device to end his narrative as he returns to the earlier bird image and provides us with a relevant but little-known fact about birds, that they have testicles, a fact that is more than just information; it is also an image and it radiates poignantly.

✎ ✎ ✎

Let's try our hand at a narrative poem. First, go into memory's vault, all the way back to childhood, and withdraw your own story of victimization and revenge. Were you bullied, did someone steal something from you, betray you, break a confidence? How did you get even? Tell that story. Dare to take pleasure in your revenge. Don't have a good story? Borrow someone else's.

As you revise, pay attention to the poetry in your narrative. Include a fanciful image early on, one that might rise to the level of symbol. Bring that image back in at the end of your poem, including some odd, little known piece of information.

Pay attention to the sounds of your story. Revise your diction to get in some alliteration and consonance.

Capitalize on some hyperbole and personification.

Bonus points for an allusion to a movie, TV show, book, or song.

An alternative: Make your narrator the perpetrator instead of the victim.

Sample Poems

Incident

I can still see it, there I was,
a third grader walking home from school
on the long, long sidewalk bordered by hedges

where Richard LaBarre, in his red parka,
jumped out of the bushes
and punched me in my stomach

so hard that I went into shock,
at first because I couldn't believe
someone would do that,

and then because it hurt like a nightmare,
sending me into a kind of trance,
off into my best Calvin and Hobbes

dream of an escape contraption
that carried me up and up
toward the clouds, the moon, and stars,

so dazed that I didn't realize
how hard I was crying
until a nice woman—my celestial guardian—

pulled over to the curb and asked me
if I'd like a ride home, but I said no because
I wasn't allowed to go with strangers.

I made my way back to my mother alone.

This morning, as I re-think the incident,
the first line of "The Cremation of Sam McGee"
keeps running through my mind.

There are indeed strange, freakish things
that are done in the midnight sun—
but also in the light of day.

And there are two strange endings to this story.
One, the next time Richard LaBarre saw me,
he looked scared, pathetic, and small.

Two, even now, up to this very moment,
I find the color red disturbing.

—Susan Gundlach

Goat Hill

There under the apple tree, bees frantic
for rotten fruit, Colleen Cunningham hit me

on the forehead with a milk bottle
at which point my runt of a brother

puffed up his 7-year-old self, let loose a swarm
of expletives ending with *I'm going to beat*

the damn hell outta you while I stood, blood
oozing into my left eye, stung by his language

so that I forgot Colleen, the neighborhood bully—
bees a bumble in my brain as my mother

who had been ironing my white seersucker
halter top bolted from the kitchen, gave my

bloody head a glance, grabbed my brother—
Mother of God, What. Did. You. Say.

while he, wild-eyed, scratched no see ums
in his hair, sure she was angry that he

might hit Colleen blurted out: *these damn*
bugs are biting the hell outta me, words

hardly out of his mouth as she grabbed
him by his shirt collar, dragged him up the steps

muttering *wheredidyougetthatlanguage?*
while I stood there, the drone of bees

a bramble, me praying—stung
by Mother who tended to other things.

                —Libby Bernardin

Top Tips: Eleven Tips for Writing Metaphors

—Ellen Bass

1. Poetry is rooted in metaphor in which we see the similarity, the oneness, in disparate things. Our society is endlessly classifying, dividing into categories. We've become very sophisticated in our ability to differentiate. But in poetry, we're being reminded of similarities. In a poem, things which are conventionally, superficially, different are revealed as being in some essential way, similar. We say, this is like that. And when it's true, when it's accurate, barriers collapse and we get a glimpse into the oneness of the world. But of course it's necessary for the metaphor to be new enough, vital enough, to actually perform this feat. So it's that fresh vision that we're trying to cultivate.

2. The best metaphors are there not just for decoration, but because metaphor is the only way we can say it. There are feelings, thoughts, and states of being that can't be written about directly and still communicate beyond the most superficial level. So to say the unsayable, we need to use other paths and metaphor is one of them.

3. Many of us operate in ruts when we look for metaphors. Thus, we wind up with an overabundance of similar, overused images. So if you seem always to be comparing things with something from your garden, look elsewhere. Look under the hood of your car, in your elementary school, in the grocery store.

4. You can look in your imagination, but you can also look literally. Go out into the world and look around. If you're trying to think of a metaphor for what it's like to caress your lover's skin or the pain of cancer or your dog's exuberance, you can take that unsolved question with you and look for its solution through your day. As you drive around town, brush your teeth, fold the laundry, keep your senses open and look, listen, smell, taste, and touch.

5. Vary scale.

6. Make lists of possible metaphors for the thing you're trying to describe. It's easier to come up with twenty or thirty ideas that don't have to be good than to find the one that's perfect. Don't judge these ideas, just brainstorm and let your mind relax and keep offering you possibilities. The right one will often be hidden in the list.

7. If you can think in metaphor as you start the first draft, that's great. But it's also possible to go back and insert metaphors in poems that could use more attention to detail and description. I think of this as the holiday ham method. You know how you take a ham and make little cuts in it and then you stick cloves into those slits? Well, that's what you do with the metaphors.

8. Galway Kinnell said, *It's okay to have something strange in your poem. In fact, it's preferable*. Be willing to be wild, to go out on a limb, to risk making a fool of yourself.

9. There's a kinetic tension between the thing and the thing it's being compared to. It's like an Escher drawing where your eye goes back and forth between figure and ground. In this way, the reader is drawn in as a participant and, unconsciously, tests the metaphor against their own experience or imagination. As Mark Doty says, *The more the yoked things do not have in common, the greater the tension*.

10. Metaphors are there to be of service. Sometimes a metaphor is too pushy and eclipses the thing being described, rather than illuminating it. In that case, it must leave.

11. Poems don't always need metaphors. Chekhov once said talent is the ability to distinguish between the *essential and inessential*.

Bonus Prompt: The Monochromatic Poem

Colors can energize a poem. Pick a single color. Make a list of ten images with that color. For example, if your color is red, your list might include a red cardinal, a bowl of red cranberries, a worm-riddled red apple, the back of a head matted with red blood.

Now use these images in a new poem.

Keep writing and revising until you feel the internal tug that signals you've found your poem.

Does your poem need more color? Or less?

Revision tip: When a draft lacks pizzazz, insert some color.

VI. Achieving Tone

If it's darkness we're having,
let it be extravagant.

—Jane Kenyon

Craft Tip #16: Tone It Up

—Peter E. Murphy

I love coming across a poem that doesn't read like any poem I've ever read before. I love the joy it inflicts on me when it does something I didn't know a poem could do, or it does something familiar in a way I hadn't thought possible. I search for more of the writer's poems hoping that kind of lightning will strike again. I want to call up the poet and thank her. I want to shake her hand. But really, I want to learn to do what she does. Call it style. Call it voice. Call it tone. This is the thing that makes our poems memorable.

Because we are the makers of these little word machines called poems, we are in charge of creating the tone for each one we compose. Robert Lowell wrote "Skunk Hour" in what he described in another poem as the *tranquilized Fifties*. Lowell, a genuine American aristocrat, describes the posh eccentricities of his fellow blue bloods. But in the middle of the poem, he interrupts his meditation to write, *My mind's not right*, which startles me every time I read it. What hootspa! What joy! My mind's not right either. Lowell's intimate gesture makes me feel like he's talking to me.

By the way, did you notice in the previous paragraph that I used both *aristocrat* and *blue bloods*? While both words mean the same thing, they dress differently. An aristocrat might wear a red robe and crown, while a blue blood could be wearing a dressing robe with a cigarette holder dangling from his fingers. Each creates a different tone. As poets, we must choose every word that we put in our poems, not just the first responders that happen to show up.

In her poem "Incendiary Art" Patricia Smith chooses words like *funk, spritzing*, and *glopped*, onomatopoetic words that make my tongue dance as I read down the page. And she uses them in service to an A-B-A rhyme scheme, rich with other luscious words such as *wanderlust, cussing, bliss*, and *skillets*, all of which add to the sound feast. And I didn't even mention *waltz to whirling sparks*. This is not a poem I'll read before turning out the light, but it will sure brighten the next day as the sun rises within me.

Jack Gilbert's "Failing and Flying" is a quiet poem that sneaks up. He uses a confident voice that tells a story I know well, but he has a surprising point of view. Not just the story of Icarus whom I know like a brother, but the story of that thing with crumbling wings, love. Gilbert reminds me, *Everyone forgets that Icarus also flew*. He's right. I forgot the glorious hours before the splash, the way I have forgotten the glorious years, and sometimes hours, before the breakups. Gilbert leads me to his conclusion, *I believe Icarus was not failing as he fell, / but just coming to the end of his triumph*. He doesn't shout, do cartwheels, or fly in circles like Icarus. He calmly prepares me to be astonished.

Hand me a Sandy Gingras poem, and even if her name's not on it, I'll know it's a Sandy Gingras poem. She writes in a deadly whimsical tone that is always original. In "Poof" she places us in the middle of an argument that includes cryogenics, microwave popcorn, and a mother who refuses to hear what her adult daughter is saying:

> On the cover, there's a picture
> of a white building with no windows.
> I tell her, I go, "I'm never gonna visit you there."

Rather than writing *I say*, she chooses the surprisingly brilliant vernacular *I tell her, I go,* and she uses *I'm never gonna* rather than the grammatical *I'm not going to*. This stuttered utterance, this hesitation, allows the speaker to process what her dearly beloved mother is up to. These gestures reveal how the speaker relates to a world that goes out of its way to confound her.

My earliest poems were dark tales told in a dark voice, but I'm done with that. This boy just wants to have fun, so I've been messing around with tone in my recent poems. "Next" begins:

> My mother, my father, and Hitler walk into a bar
> where I am the bartender. I'm not dead yet,
> so they don't recognize me.

I've set myself up for a joke which I hope will be funny, if you can call anything to do with Hitler funny. Okay, Mel Brooks's *The Producers* is a hoot.

"Next" welcomes outrageous characters, including a shy sunbeam, a dapper cockroach on the make, a pair of militaristic eagles, and a fire-breathing dragon, each of whom shares a line break and sometimes a drink with the Führer. Before concluding, however, the poem turns serious, keeping in mind Frost's dictum that a poem *begins in delight and ends in wisdom.*

> Why have I always doubted where I've come from?
> What does your name mean?
> What have any of us ever done to deserve this life?

If our poems sound like everyone else's poems, we may be good, but we'll be forgettable. We need to take risks in diction, subject matter, and form. We need to make deliberate gestures that reveal our inner nurturer or our inner freak or our inner blue blood. We need to experiment with words and phrases so our poems sound more like our inner us, unique and uniquely crafted.

Poem and Prompt

But It Was an Accident

Yes, I was the one who left out the open petri dishes of polio
and plague next to the plate of pasta.

I leaked the nuclear codes, the ones on giant floppy disks from 1982.
I fell asleep at the button. I ordered tacos and turned out the lights.
How was I to know that someone was waiting for the right time?

I thought the radio was saying "Alien attack"
and headed for the fallout shelter, failing to feed the dogs.

I followed evacuation plans. I just followed orders.
I was the pilot of the bomber, I was the submarine captain,
I steered into the iceberg. I held the scalpel but I was shaking.
I was the one in charge. I was on the red phone saying "Do it" decisively.

I always imagined writing propaganda; how could I possibly see
what was coming when they dropped the fliers,
when the angry mobs began choking people in the street?
I was always good at creating a panic.

I never saw the Ferris wheel start its fatal roll.
I looked away just as the plane plummeted,
as the building burned. I shook my head at disaster, afraid to meet.

It was just an accident. It was fate. It was never my hand on the wheel.
When you point fingers, point them towards the empty sky.

—Jeannine Hall Gailey

In this *mea culpa* poem, Gailey's speaker claims responsibility for all manner of serious misfortunes, e.g., causing the polio epidemic, leaking the nuclear codes, piloting the bomber plane. Of course, this catalogue is hyperbolic; we know that one person alone was not responsible for all the speaker claims credit for.

The tone is intriguing. Is the speaker bragging or apologizing? And there's irony in the tone as well. Who would claim credit for doing such terrible things?

Note the seemingly inappropriate touch of humor as Gailey effectively employs *zeugma*, i.e., the juxtaposition of the serious with the trivial as in the opening lines: *Yes, I was the one who left out the open petri dishes of polio / and plague next to the plate of pasta.* Then after she leaked the nuclear codes, the speaker ordered tacos.

The poem gains power from its use of anaphora in the many sentences that begin with *I* followed by a verb. The poem also gains power from the poet's use of plosives, particularly the letter *p*. Look at the string of words containing a *p* in just the first two lines: *open, petri, polio, plague, plate, pasta*—and then throughout the rest of the poem.

A surprising turn occurs in the penultimate stanza as the speaker turns away from what she claims to have caused and instead denies culpability and blames it all on accident and fate.

✐ ✐ ✐

For your own *mea culpa* poem, first generate a list of misdeeds, misfortunes, and disasters. Create a mixture of global and local.

Begin your draft by getting right up in our faces with your bold claim of responsibility. Do not be wishy-washy. Be hyperbolic. Keep the draft going, line after line, until you've depleted your list.

Now go over your draft and add in some trivial misdeeds, just a few. Zeugma is a very effective technique but should be used gingerly. If used wisely, it adds humor and by contrast draws attention to the serious item. If overused, it loses its subtlety and surprise and diminishes the weight of the serious item.

Towards the end of your poem, bring in a turn, something that surprises both you and the reader.

As you revise, pay attention to sentence structure and sounds. Play with *p, b, k, t* sounds. Make diction choices to get better sounds. You might want to choose a single sound and let it predominate throughout the poem.

Sample Poems

Humble Pie

Here we are again, the evening after an argument,
both of us eating the entrails, picking around the edges
of the liver with our forks, not entirely sure we want to
eat the heart, but knowing the way inoculation works,
the way we must take inside of ourselves a little of what hurts
in order to become stronger. It's never about who didn't
water the garden, wash the plate, smooth the bed, close the window.
It's not even about the soaked sill, the dried stalks.
I'm ashamed to say it's because I am overtired and righteous
and you are quick to draw and thirsty for control. Oh, my love,
I plan to never leave. Let the kings and queens eat the venison.
Our union has made servants of us, and I'm happy for the leavings
we swallow together, a mug of your homemade beer to wash
them down, my hand on your sinewy leg under the table.

—Rebecca Hart Olander

Getaway Car

I ran two red lights after the last time I met him
in a motel because my life seemed more
like a movie that way—easier to cut

away to the scene where a North Korean general
holds a pistol to some nuclear physicist's temple
in one of those rooms with steel beams

and low lights, where fate is strung out, tenuous,
flickering—and you've got to come up with the goods or else.
How many years did I plan my escape?

But who wants to face the room where she's left the best
part of herself behind? Half a world away
an award-winning journalist thought she'd blend in

wearing old dungarees and a shirt that wasn't vinylon
but she forgot to secure the Dear Leader's pin over her heart.
Yeah, I could've robbed a bank, wrapped my hand

in a paper bag and pretended I'd shoot. The money
would come in handy. I could travel, meet someone
else, fall in love. But only one road runs through this town

and just cause you drive fast doesn't mean you can get out.
Sometimes what's true in life is also true
in the movies: Like when blindfolded hostages nod

their heads, tap, tap, tapping in some jailbird code
to the cell next door where a journalist who's chronicled
all our misdeeds is lying in a pool of her

own piss, right where we've left her.

—Andrea Bates

164

Craft Tip #17: Key-Change as Poetic Device

—Christopher Salerno

First, you may want to go listen to a few songs: Michael Jackson's "Man in the Mirror," REM's "Stand," The Ramones' "I Want to Be Sedated," or The Talking Heads' "And She Was."

These songs have in common that they contain, mid-song, a change of key. Loosely transferable to the medium of poetry, a key-change in a poem involves an instance that, whether lasting for a significant part of the poem or just for a short time, signals a shift, a ramping up, a moving on, a rally, a diversion, or an alternate pitch. The overall tone of an early draft we are writing may be in danger of flattening to the point that the poem bores the reader or else presents only one emotional register. Think about the effect of reading several dozen tautly-formed, end-stopped lines of iambic pentameter—after a while the meter and form feel monotonous. And while flatness or regularity is not always a bad thing, I can say that my favorite modern poems are quite often those that have the ability to startle me a little by employing one of the following devices that serve to change the key in a poem:

1. Great Question(s)

I would argue that the best poems are written by the poet with more questions than answers. Often as we write a draft, one or more central questions linger behind the core argument or investigation happening in the poem. And so it's more than organic for these questions to make their way into our poems. Consider H.D.'s "Sea Violet" for an example of the emergence of the poem's core question: *The greater blue violets / flutter on the hill, / but who would change for these...?* Such moments can change the poem's key right away. Read Robinson Jeffers' "Love the Wild Swan" or Robert Creeley's "The Rain" for examples of how a question can change the entire direction of the poem.

2. Flash-Formalism

Random passages of iambic, trochaic, anapestic, or dactylic lines can create an almost passionate moment in a poem. Deliberately simplifying or minimizing sentence size and structure at certain moments can jostle any poem. Read Lorine Niedecker's "[Well, Spring Overflows the Land]" and you will see how a poem which operates in one manner for the first eight lines can suddenly starch its posture and finish with five short, end-stopped, declarative sentences. Langston Hughes's well-known poem, "The Weary Blues," likewise seems to shift its key in the final five lines by abandoning the jazz phrasing that dominates the first thirty lines and moving into a passage of structured syllabic lines. This startles the reader into increased attention. As with a song changing its key midway, if the listener's mind has been wandering, it is brought back to the surface by this shift.

3. Epiphany

Some lyric poems serve as a record of discovery, epiphany, or transcendence. See the final lines of Rilke's "Archaic Torso of the Apollo" or James Wright's "Lying in a Hammock at William Duffy's Farm in Pine Island, Minnesota." Both of these poems (James Wright may ultimately owe Rilke a few bucks for this one) capture their speakers' processes as they reach an epiphany. What may also be on display here are the vestigial bits of the sonnet where the volta repositions the poem's central thought or argument culminating in a changing of attention or tone. Of course, as poets we are always trying to open ourselves to moments where we are so moved by our subject that we blossom on the page. A definite change of key!

4. Enjambment

Tasteful enjambment can always be used to heighten attention and startle the reader. Risking a little bit more with your line breaks at a key point in the poem or shifting the orderliness of certain lines can serve as a key-change in the poem. A masterful example can be found in William Carlos Williams' "Spring and All," which jars the reader a bit with its line breaks but does so when the subject of the poem (the messy emergence of spring) demands it (form follows content). The business of making and breaking lines can be for some as measured as the art of French cuisine. In Frank O'Hara's poem "To the Harbormaster," we see how a master of the conversational poetic voice uses this device to establish and then heighten that voice in the middle of the poem. It begins with a relatively conventional use of enjambment, but over the course of the poem's seventeen lines, there are some very angular, sharp-edged enjambments that cause the reader to pay special attention at the end of the line as if one were walking along some high ridge whose path has suddenly narrowed.

Ultimately, if we see that poems, like songs, tend to establish themselves in a dominant key, then we can ask ourselves just how dynamic an experience we are creating for the reader. It's more than okay to break some of the aesthetic promises set up earlier in the poem, especially when the result may draw attention to a shift in the poem, keep or change the reader's interest, or, hopefully, truly deepen it.

Poem and Prompt

Traveler's Lament

> *Should we have stayed home and dreamed of here?*
> *Where should we be today?*
> —"Questions of Travel," Elizabeth Bishop

I miss the man who sells us wine, suggests
the Covey Run,

Rainbow Grocery's neon orange tennis ball
tangerine stacks.

I miss the flower shop with its bundles of African Daisies,
Queen Anne's Lace.

I miss our street, gossamer blossoms stuck like unlucky insects
to windshields, headlights.

I even miss the neighbor's pick-up truck turning over, at six am,
twenty Hoovers and a leaf blower,

clang of dumpster lid. Futility of sweeping sunflower hulls
from the walk,

the mailman bringing (politely, daily) more and more
of nothing.

I miss lugging the trash to the curb in a robe
about to slip open,

the hot water tank we easily emptied
each time we made love in the tub.

—Martha Silano

In her list poem, Silano catalogs what the speaker misses back home while she's visiting somewhere else. The poet begins with a title that does double duty; the poem is indeed a lamentation for what's missed, for what's causing her homesickness, but it's also a praise poem for what makes home a sweet place.

Let's consider the structural devices. Silano uses anaphora. Each new sentence begins with *I miss* with only one variation which occurs in stanza 5 as the poet inserts *even* into *I miss*. This small insertion lets us know that it's the small things she misses, not the big ones.

Silano gives us nine stanzas, consisting of a total of five sentences. Each stanza is divided into two lines, a good choice as two places are included as well as two lovers. Within the five sentences, some items get listed and then broken down into details, e.g., in stanza 3 the speaker misses the flower shop and then specifies *its bundles of African Daisies, / Queen Anne's Lace.*

As the poem proceeds, the poet moves from one sense to another. Stanza 1 hits on taste with its reference to wine, stanza 2 appeals to our sense of sight as we see a stack of tangerines, stanzas 5 and 6 zero in on our sense of sound with their references to a noisy truck and a clang. And surely the last stanza appeals to our sense of touch.

That closing stanza is where the poem turns, so subtly and cleverly. But notice how Silano prepares us for the turn in the preceding stanza 8 as she introduces the speaker's *robe / about to slip open*, then moves to the hot water tank and the bathtub where she and her partner made love. Now that's just delicious.

✐ ✐ ✐

Let's do a lamentation poem that employs a list structure. You might also do a traveler's lament, but perhaps you'd rather try another topic, perhaps a divorcée's lament, a widow's lament, a parent's lament, a pet lover's lament, a dieter's lament. Let your speaker miss what's no longer available.

Begin by brainstorming a list of about ten things your speaker would miss about your subject if or when separated from it.

Begin drafting your poem. Consider using anaphora as a structural device, one which will also add music to your poem.

Go for the sensory appeals, covering several of the senses. As Silano does, toss in a few metaphors or similes.

Work for the turn, the key-change, in that final part of your poem, something that will surprise your readers—and hopefully you, too.

Can you get in a touch of irony? Perhaps complain about what you really liked.

Sample Poems

Missing

I miss the very first chirping of birds,
the nonstop cardinal we hear through the day.

I miss the routine of who is first in the bathroom,
of who does which chores, long-established routine.

I miss the brown earthy taste of our coffee,
just as we like it, that lasts through the morning.

I even miss the dish soap smell by the sink,
the dirty clothes hamper and compost pail mess.

I miss the green, evergreens and maples, welcome
tunnel of trees when I pull in the driveway.

I miss our garden, your shoveling, my troweling,
the battle with bugs, the long growing, sweet harvest.

I miss our usual comings and goings, barely a need
for our quick-scribbled fridge notes after so many years.

I miss dappled light on the path where we walk,
the last light of day on the tops of the hemlocks.

I miss the night gurgle of frogs in the pond—
occasional bass gollop, a comma in the chorus.

And the motion of the mattress when you come to bed
whether I wake or make it into a dream.

—Elizabeth Bodien

Tennis Player's Lament

The art of losing isn't hard to master.
—Elizabeth Bishop

I miss the clay courts. Thick red dirt.
    Terracotta stains on my skirt's ball-pockets.
        Canvas tennis shoes clumped

with dirt. I miss the all-white palette of wooly socks,
    regulation Bermuda shorts, cable-knit sweaters,
        collared shirts & crocodile logo.

I miss my wooden Dunlop, woven with cow-gut,
    triangular frame, screws tight against warping.
        Wilson tin cans lined on shelves in Cowan's

Athletic store on Main. Just yesterday, I breathed
    the freshly opened
can of tennis. I yearn to hear the pinging
    back and forth across the net.

I miss those vanishing
    summers strung together like
        an endless game.

I miss the overheads, backhands,
    and drop shots, Fila dress & racquet,
        a buckler and sword.

Alone in my room, I long for
    my poachable moments. My losses
        buried back there.

Still in communion with the art of tennis,
I imagine the game, a stylized dance of love. Matisse
understood. The tumbles,
the leaps, the stops, and starts,

the springing, the flourishes. The celebration
of sky, earth, and body, wheeling and twisting—
I miss the elements in unity. I miss the dust caked beneath

my fingernails,
red clay in
the creases of my fingers.

—Deborah Gerrish

Craft Tip #18: Asphyxiating the Silence in Your Neck of the Woods: On the Importance of Speech Tones

—Adrian Blevins

W. H. Auden says that *poetry just may be defined as the clear expression of mixed feelings* because poems have to say more than they say because being double-minded is what makes poems *poems*. There are many methods and techniques for meaning more than you say, but my favorite is to work with varying levels of diction by merging the spoken with the written. It's an especially southern trick that I first heard from my favorite novelists and short story writers like Barry Hannah, Lewis Nordan, Eudora Welty, and others.

In the first chapter of Lewis Nordan's great novel *Wolf Whistle*, Alice Conroy asks Mr. Archer, the school's vice principal, to let her take her fourth grade class into the "Balance Due" neighborhood of Arrow Catcher, Mississippi, to visit their injured classmate, Glen Gregg. Here's the narration of Mr. Archer pondering his decision to let Alice take her young students into a neighborhood where a "Nazi voodoo woman" incidentally asks Alice if she's "the Lard Jesus":

> If it were any other teacher on the staff, Mr. Archer declared, he wouldn't allow it, he simply would not. Never on this earth would he allow fifteen nine-year-olds to walk into Balance Due, even in the early morning, no way, not a chance, no siree bobtail. He was making a mistake, he said, he knew it, it was against his better judgment, he shouldn't allow it, he didn't know what was in his mind, he ought to have his head examined.

By including the reader in a speech act whose actual literal meaning seems far less important than the unequivocal rhythm generated by that hilarious string of negations—*no way, not a chance, no siree bobtail*—this passage cuts the distance separating the text from the reader (a distance I think writers ought to break their very necks to minimize). The speech tones here are inherently friendly and welcoming and outgoing and no-nonsense. And the use of idioms—*never on this earth, it was against his better judgment*, and *he ought to have his head examined*—all characterize Mr. Archer and emphasize the situational irony governing the whole passage, since Alice *does* end up taking her fourth graders into Balance Due only to find out by actually seeing Glenn under bandages in his bed that he *would soon be dead if he was lucky*.

How we feel about our speakers is even more important in poetry. The insight that gets Bob Hicok's "Elegy's" going—that the word *elegy* sounds like and even *is* like the word *eulogy*—generates an association with that other formal, public, and often religious ceremony, the wedding, which generates the phrase *dearly beloved*, which then turns on the major differences between a wedding where groups are *gathered together* and a death, where people, the speaker tells us, *are un-gathered*:

> Elegy's
>
> almost eulogy, is nearly dearly
> beloved, I am un-gathered here
> where you are not, I confess
> I obsess, repeat myself to feel
> this speaking's more than the creaking
> of a pew in an empty church, where
> as a tyke, surrounded by an absence
> I was priestly asked to think of
> as love, I couldn't wrap my mind
> around such a zilch, whereas you
> I touch and smell in the rough flesh
> of memory, the word sonically
> wants to be remember me, in my head
> at least, you thrive some, you die some
> daily in this weird-ass and misty mix
> of ghost and gone, to which
> I address what pretends to be
> litany but is no more
> evolved than this stuck
> list: come back, come home

Notice in this poem of many repetitions—all those *ly* sounds; the repetition of exact words and syntactic structures; the rhymes. What a pleasure the words *tyke* and *zilch* are, like little bits of candy in the mouth. Poems are made up of patterns—let's call them echoes—and surprises—let's call these ruptures—and the words *tyke* and *zilch* are fish out of water here because they're more spoken than written. They animate us to the myriad possibilities of language and tell us like a little slap on the face that anything might happen next. They say, wake up! This is important because it's *actual talk.*

The *weird-ass and misty mix* of the sounds of *tyke* and *zilch* in a poem that also contains so many sonorous repetitions and more formal words like *litany* and legalese like *whereas* creates what I call a *texture* that makes the poem's soundscape audible the way that linen and wool are more touchable because they have multiple levels to actually feel whereas a fabric like polyester is just too even and flat to sufficiently touch and therefore sense and know. In addition to pointing to the idea of nothing being there—"Elegy's," after all, an elegy, and the speaker is meditating in these lines on the idea of an invisible God that he couldn't *wrap [his] mind around* when he was young—the words *tyke* and *zilch* remind us that language is funny and unpredictable and, well, a little wild. A little squally and windswept.

Jorie Graham says that we *must be memorable or not at all.* Though I've concentrated mostly on poetry here, I think this advice might also apply to prose writers and filmmakers and actors and doctors and belly dancers and dogs in parks with nannies pushing prams. The trick to me no matter the genre is to asphyxiate the silence with patterns and surprises or patterns of surprise or however you say it in your neck of the woods. There are lots of ways of doing it, but getting the words back into the mouth without being grotesquely predictable is what I notice most when I'm reading a sentence I not only can hear but *want* to hear because we really don't know what's going to happen next, do we? And time's running short and the world is too much with us and all of that.

Poem and Prompt

Fantastic Voyage

> *Methought what pain it was to drown.*
> —Richard III, Shakespeare

My bladder stone looks like the coral reef
I snorkeled over, terrified, last summer.
It's crystal white, a prickly sphere, embedded
deep in my bladder wall. What a treat
to lie propped on a pillow on a gurney
watching a TV screen display my innards
beamed up by a camera submarine
instead of breathing through a narrow tube
while keeping afloat in fifty feet of water
and peering downward through fogged diving goggles.
No brilliant branches, yellow, red, and green,
relieve the monochrome of calcium,
but thousands of small spikes grow from my stone
intricate, symmetrical as a gem.
The microscopic camera swoops and pans,
projecting images like Jacques Cousteau's,
minus shoals of blue and golden fish
such as the ones I saw weave through the reef,
breathing water while I gasped for air.
How I wished that I were one of them,
aswim in water rich in oxygen,
breathing through my gills, taking in
the beauty I'd crossed continents to see.
This beauty inside of me's much easier
to take in. But, like the reef, it's threatened.
It must come out tomorrow or I'll drown
slowly in my poisons. Not intact,

but smashed to fragments small enough to exit
the narrow tube through which it must be passed.
It's kill or be killed, my lovely, spiky stone,
my finest work of art. Hail and farewell!

—Richard Cecil

The title of Cecil's poem sets us up for the nautical analogy that runs throughout the poem and structures it. The epigraph furthers the preparation. Then the first line makes a comparison between the speaker's bladder stone and a coral reef he explored last summer. The analogy is then exploited throughout the poem as the first-person speaker compares and contrasts the two and provides descriptive details for both.

The tone of the poem is intriguing. It's conversational. It is also understated and ironic. The speaker finds his bladder stone interesting but not especially alarming. He declares, *What a treat / to lie propped on a pillow on a gurney / watching a TV screen display my innards...* A treat? Hardly. He suggests that this kind of exploration he's now observing is better than the kind he engaged in last summer. That, too, seems unlikely.

The poet employs some metaphors to illuminate his subject. The camera that explores his innards is a *submarine*. His bladder stone is *symmetrical as a gem*. At the end of the poem, the stone is characterized as the speaker's *finest work of art*.

Notice the poet's use of color. The coral reef is full of color— yellow, red, and green—and is surrounded by blue and golden fish. On the other hand, the stone is characterized by its absence of color. It's crystal white (a *monochrome of calcium*), has no brilliant branches in various colors, and has no colorful fish.

The speaker employs direct address at the end of the poem as he says, *It's kill or be killed, my lovely, spiky stone...* Then he offers the traditional military greeting and farewell when a new commander is replaced by an old one: *Hail and farewell!*

Let's try a poem based on an analogy. Begin with this starter line: "My _____ looks like _____."

Fill in the first blank with some undesirable physical attribute, e.g., your rotten tooth, a pimple, ingrown toenail, hernia, ruptured appendix. Then ask yourself, What does this remind me of? What might you compare and contrast your item with? Put that in the second blank.

Jot down some descriptive details for both items in your analogy.

Begin with your starter line and keep going, adding in and alternating the descriptive details for the two items. Bring in some colors.

Add some snazzy metaphors.

Use a direct address towards the end of your poem. How does that perk up the poem?

Bonus points for an epigraph taken from another work of literature.

Sample Poems

On Bended Knee

She almost wrote the words down on her knee...
—"Maple," Robert Frost

My knees look like two deflated brown balloons—
released from air that kept them taut.
My two once worked the crop fields,
like Mamá, whose knees were
duplicate-size mine; the ones she
prayed on daily; forced mine to join
her on cold cement floor.
Balloons come in endless shades—my
knees know only one—turn
darker in the sun.

Over time, my saggy knees
mirror an elephant's—whose
body mirrors a gargantuan deflated
balloon. My mother-in-law got her knee
replaced; it ballooned to twice its size
before it healed; took weeks
before she could bend
it; for months, needed a cane
to help her get around.
Her arthritic hands could not be
replaced; her knees learned
how to bend for prayer: ask
to be released from joint pain.

Balloons can be bent
into animal shapes with four knees—
blessed be the beasts who feed us,
so we can take our knees to work and play.

Cousins to my big knees,
my elbows don't carry my weight,
but do keep me afloat in pool
or high water.

My boomerang-shaped knees are joined
to me to the end, unlike balloons
released to drift into the gentle air.

—Anjela Villarreal Ratliff

In Media Res

When I consider how my light is spent...
—"On His Blindness," John Milton

Milton, at 30, visited Galileo Galilei, already old and blind,
to learn the solar system, the stars, the Two World Systems.
This was before his own blindness, before paradise was lost.
Galileo, arrested, forced to recant that Earth circles the sun.
Milton, before him three marriages, four children, a rich life
that probably led to glaucoma, and as his lens to the world
became Galileo's telescope from the wrong end, asked God
and Satan how things had gone so wrong in human affairs.

This, my own quatorzain on damaged optic nerves
that slowly take my peripheral view into a tunnel,
narrowing my focus to a straight-ahead vision,
making me reconsider how my light is spent,
writing while I can see, then amanuensis like John,
'til what remains is blank verse of a paradise regained.

—Kenneth Ronkowitz

Top Tips: How to Write It Bloody

—Jan Beatty

Start pulling on the rope inside you, the wild *no* that lives
    in the unspoken place,
and see what comes when you pull.

Feel the past voices that you don't want to hear, feel the thing
    that you'll never say—no,
not ever, to anyone. Start writing those voices.

Put the body in. Arms, eyes, face, body parts.

Don't just narrate an activity. We need to *feel* it.

Go back to the rope and pull it again.

Write down any stray words or bits that come to you, whether
    or not they make sense.

Don't make it nice, don't make it sweet.

Avoid solving a puzzle. Avoid making everything neat and tidy.

Make the biggest mess of words you can. Free associate
    with this mess until you can't write anymore.

Don't edit. Feel the terror of what you're writing/
keep going.

Don't worry about who will read it/like it/hate it/need it.
This is *your* rope, *your* poem.

Pull the rope again and start to feel more coming.
Feel the flip side of terror/discovery.

Give us nouns. Kill the adjectives. Kill the clever.

Now you're getting inside the body, the ultimate domestic space.
Let it cover you, let it blur and change you.

What would happen if you loved the thing that scourges?

If you loved the thing that tears you open?

Love it now, and write it messy, write it bloody.
Love it so you can see it, call it out, shred it, own it, own it hard.
Put the body in.

Pull the rope.

Bonus Prompt: The Monosyllabic Poem

Write a poem consisting entirely of one-syllable words. A line might look like this:

A band of dirt sat on his neck.

The red scarf waved in the air like a flag.

The value of the monosyllable is its force. Be sure you have lots of stressed syllable words to enhance the rhythm. A string of them creates a pounding rhythm. On the other hand, a string of unstressed syllables in a row results in flatness.

Later, of course, you may choose to make some substitutions. That's fine as it's usually a good idea to break a pattern.

VII. Dealing with Feelings

*I like the feeling of being about to confront
an experience and resolve it as art.*

—Eudora Welty

Craft Tip #19: Sentimentality, Character, and the Health of Your Poem

—Patrick Donnelly

Since most poetry aspires to express feeling, especially strong feeling, every poet needs to learn how to recognize the phenomenon of sentimentality—a tonal imbalance that can completely disable a poem—and develop strategies for dealing with it.

Subjects in which there seems to reside an inherent undertow toward sentimentality are, in general, topics about which the writer experiences extreme subjectivity, and/or topics around which there is a danger of too much sweetness or melodrama. Specifically, writing about: a beloved child, aged relative, or pet (or the suffering, sickness or death of any of these). Other such topics include: spiritual or religious subjects, a nostalgic memory of happiness or sadness, natural beauty, patriotism, a public tragedy, or triumph over adversity.

It's not that you don't *go* there—you do, you must—but you enter the arena alert to the risks, and ready to deploy the antidotes to sentimentality in various combinations.

If we think of sentimentality, or a tendency in that direction, as a kind of wet, soft, squishy influence on the poem, we need something dry, hard, and unyielding to hold it up and counter that influence. A tendency toward sentimentality—a poem that goes right to that edge, or even over the edge—can be turned into an aesthetic asset, if engineered properly. There's a saying that the sins of the hot-blooded will be judged on a different scale than those of the cold-hearted, and I personally prefer poetry that risks sentimentality to poetry that is relentlessly opaque, distant, mental, ironic, smart-assed, and cold. But both approaches have their dangers, and both must be skillfully managed for the health of the poem.

Here's where it can get complicated: *people* are occasionally sentimental, and there's absolutely no reason a writer can't create a sentimental character, including the speaker, in a poem.

But remember that the speaker or character can be sentimental without the poem itself being so. The poem can use some devices to acknowledge, or distance itself from, a character's sentimentality.

One aspect that differentiates sentimental writing from writing that isn't sentimental is how tensions are resolved. In sentimental writing, serious tension is either not allowed to arise at all or is resolved in ways that are not often mirrored in life. Poems that are not sentimental allow tensions both to arise and to continue unresolved beyond the ending of the poem, which in turn allows the poem itself to continue to resonate in the reader's thoughts and feelings.

Of course, audiences trained to expect sentimentality in poetry, and to prefer it, may be made uncomfortable by unsentimental poetry—perhaps in ways they couldn't articulate—and may actually prefer not to have the poem continue to resonate, especially in the case of uncomfortable thoughts and feelings. We have all gone away from certain movies angry, for instance, at a certain level of unresolved mystery—it's human nature to long for *closure*. But if one takes a good look at the world, lack of closure is perhaps its primary quality.

Here, from my own struggle with this topic, are some influences that can balance poetic gestures or tones of voice that tend toward the sentimental, that can, in effect, toughen up the poem:

1. Acerbity, pungency, tartness, or even dryness, because sentimentality is usually sweet, bland, cloying and damp. Also wit, irony, humor, or sarcasm, because exercise of these implies a degree of distance.

2. Understatement, distance, coldness, or sangfroid, because sentimentality, melodrama, and special-pleading (*You can never fully understand my pain, because it's worse than your pain, and deserves more attention*) are bosom buddies. Melodrama aids and abets sentimentality, and vice versa, because each operates with stock, stereotypical characters and narrative clichés. Understatement often achieves far more than laying it on with a trowel.

3. Syntactical interest and elegance, formal or intellectual rigor (or any kind of rigor) because the human faculty that creates structural integrity also requires and nurtures an editorial distance that is antidote to the subjectivity of sentimentality. Sentimental writers too often want the writing to be appreciated primarily for *what* it reports about their lived experience, and don't give enough attention to *how* it reports.

4. Precision and specificity, because sentimentality often goes hand in hand with nonspecificity, abstraction, and blandness. The facts of the world, carefully observed, honestly and precisely described, are never sentimental.

5. Freshness and surprise, because sentimentality traffics in cliché, both of language and overall concept, and in obviousness. It takes time, distance, and investigation to push past what Ellen Bryant Voigt has called *clichés of perception [and] clichés of expression*. Clichés of expression are easy enough to catch; you can train yourself to scan your writing, root those out and replace them with fresher language. But clichés of perception are harder to discover, because we have to have, first of all, the distance and humility to recognize that we might be *susceptible* to clichés of perception, then the persistence to penetrate to deeper levels of perception.

6. Weirdness, strangeness, uncanniness, or grotesquerie, because sentimentality is profoundly reactionary, and feeds off an addiction to the status quo, the conventional, the normal and orthodox, to inoffensive prettiness rather than real beauty (which can be destabilizing), and often ignores the strangeness in the ordinary.

7. Complexity, disorder, or even messiness (a successful, *intelligible* complexity, I mean, or a vital messiness), because sentimentality often assumes a phony simplicity, a refusal to explore contradictions or challenges to its point of view, or imposes an order which is superficial or merely decorative rather than organic and load-bearing.

Sentimentality is often, on some level, an attempt to ignore or suppress disorderly passion or electricity and sometimes to favor the head over the body.

8. Darkness, danger, and risk, because sentimentality often results from a refusal to acknowledge any dark or negative potential in the topic.

9. Acknowledgment of real vulnerability, embarrassment, character flaws, or complicity with injustice, because sentimentality is often concerned to present the speaker as a sensitive and completely admirable experiencer of vicissitudes and epiphanies (an example of a cliché of perception), rather than as a person with sometimes contradictory and even ignoble impulses.

10. Ambivalence, incertitude, doubt, and ambiguity, because sentimentality traffics in certainty, preachiness, and the imperative voice.

11. Musical language, which speaks to the senses and the unconscious, because sentimentality often ignores those faculties in the reader, or prefers not to invoke them, by staying safely prosy and heady.

Poem and Prompt

Abandoned Block Factory, Arkansas

All that is left
unaccounted for:
elegance married
to rust. On the roof, rain
dwelling in the corrugations.
Some slats vanished
altogether, a blankness
giving way to sky. But the eaves
hold in perfect vertices,
refuse to abandon
their beauty, hard-earned.
High on the yellow silo,
the conveyor's lattice
is as finely wrought
as a string instrument's
struts and braces: precision
in every coordinate
and all across the godlike slant
from tower to the ground.
There would be no time at all
if not for moss swelling
in concrete cracks,
the guard rails papered
by lichen. If not for the rest
of the world, the silence
it attempts to punctuate:
crow caw. Engine roar.
Horns of every pitch
and color. The train's
shuddering Doppler,
crossing us now—as always—

in near-perfect intervals. Even
though there is no tangible
good to stop for,
nothing whole to take away.

—Elizabeth Lindsey Rogers

The title of this poem identifies the subject and its location. What follows is a poem of description. If it were that and only that, we'd feel let down. But Rogers gives her poem heft and elevates it beyond mere description by creating a distinctive tone. We feel sorrow and emptiness, almost as if a death has occurred, and yet we also feel reverence for the dilapidated building.

Notice that the poem is written from a purely objective point of view. There is no *I*, no *he, she*, or *they*, no *you*. The absence of a voice creates a sense of coldness; there's no one for us to warm up to.

However, with her descriptive details, Rogers gives us an appealing image of the building. We see *rain / dwelling in the corrugations*, then *the conveyor's lattice /... as finely wrought / as a string instrument's / struts and braces*, and *moss swelling / in concrete cracks, / the guard rails papered / by lichen*. We begin to feel something for the building.

The poet's use of contrast is essential to the poem's tone. Although the building has fallen into a terrible state of disrepair, the speaker admires its construction; once it stood in architectural beauty. Notice the simple but powerful metaphor that describes the building as *elegance married / to rust*—two opposites coming together. The blankness of the building now gives way to sky, but the *eaves / hold in perfect vertices, / refuse to abandon / their beauty*. There is silence all around the abandoned factory, but beyond the building, the noise of the world goes on: *crow caw, Engine roar, Horns*, and the clatter of a train. The inactivity of the factory is contrasted with the energy that surrounds it; the train has nothing to pick up there, but it does elsewhere, so it keeps on moving.

Rogers also uses negative terms to create contrast and tone: *no time at all*, *if not* (used twice), *no tangible good to stop for*, and *nothing whole*. These help to convey a feeling of emptiness.

Notice the contribution that diction makes to the tone of the poem. While words such as *vanished and blankness* suggest absence and loss, others suggest admiration: *perfect vertices*, *beauty*, *hard-earned*, *finely wrought*, and *precision*. The word *godlike* suggests reverence.

Ironically, the poet's use of contrast creates a sense of balance, a sense that's augmented by paired alliterative words. These are lightly scattered throughout the poem so that they remain subtle and unobtrusive: *roof, rain, Some slate, concrete cracks, crow caw*. These pairs are interspersed with non-alliterative pairs: *struts and braces, pitch and color*.

✎ ✎ ✎

We've all seen the city and the countryside littered with signs of decay. There's rich material there. Let's do a poem about something that's been abandoned and left to fall apart. Choose a subject, e.g., a ghost mall, an out-of-use roller coaster, a defunct hotel or motel, a closed restaurant, a junked car or school bus, a condemned house, a dead train car.

If possible, visit your site and spend some time just observing. If you can't visit, perhaps a photo will do. Or you can rely on your memory.

Make a list of descriptive details.

Now make a list of the feelings your subject evokes. Aim for conflicting feelings to add texture to your poem's tone. Your list might include words like *sad, forlorn, happy, festive, chaotic*.

Begin your draft. Using your descriptive details, create an image of your subject. Make us see it. Make us feel it—without telling us how to feel. Avoid using the words in your list of feelings. Let the images do the work. Keep your poem free of sentimentality.

Work in some contrasts—the beautiful and the ugly, the majestic and the decrepit. Convey the glory days and the hard times.

As you move to subsequent drafts, pay attention to diction. Find the best words to describe your subject and evoke feelings about it.

Work in some alliterative pairs. Use a light touch. Don't overdo it.

One additional challenge: try to write your poem from a purely objective point of view—no *I*, no *he, she,* or *they,* no *you.*

Sample Poems

Fifteen-mile School, Wasco County

Metal pipes for swings,
an unpainted outhouse
leaning into the wheatfield.

Is it wind from the canyon
or shrill voices of children
shaking the loose boards?

On the whitewashed wall
a tall unbroken blackboard
erased for the last time.

No glass in the windows.
Swallows up in the tower
instead of a school bell.

Nests and white streaks
from decades of nestlings
fledged from this tower.

Fallen to the dirt cellar,
scraps of notebook paper
turned almost into earth.

Whose fingers perfected
Palmer method letters
on pages with printed lines?

Down beyond Kelly Cutoff
an old stove-up rancher
longs for the school marm.

—Penelope Scambly Schott

Holy Land, USA

Who comes now but a few late-age seekers
who brave the "closed" and "no trespassing" signs
to enter the crumbling stone gate
to these seventeen desolate acres on top of a hill?
A miniature Bethlehem fallen to ruin,
the folly or passion of the Christian attorney
who erected it here sixty years ago
of cement, cast-off plywood, chicken wire,
parts of discarded stoves and refrigerators,
old stone statues, whatever he could gather
and find a use for. Once, in the 60's.
44,000 tourists came. What's left?

Tiny houses, statues, some reduced to rubble.
A weatherworn stone that says Solomon's Temple,
The partly toppled Tower of Babel,
the Last Supper diorama in cement
shattered by vandals. A partially effaced
tablet: "Jesus is condemned to death."
And the forty-six foot high-tech steel cross
that stands looking down over all of Waterbury,
I-84, and the still busy Brass Hill Mall.
There is a haunted air.
The grass and weeds grow high.
The eerie presence of the teenage girl
once murdered here.

What urge calls the rare tourist to this
desolate place? Is it simply curiosity?
What, if anything, is preserved?
Is there some sense of sacredness that remains?
A squirrel skitters as if playing around the stones,
birds arrow and veer across a vibrant sky,
the air fills with the music of their calls.
Broken beer bottles capture and flash the light.

—Patricia Fargnoli

Craft Tip #20: When Trees Talk and Boats Swagger

—Betsy Sholl

Personification, loosely defined as attributing human qualities to abstractions and animate or inanimate objects, is a figure of speech we tend to be wary of, and for good reason. John Ruskin coined the term *pathetic fallacy* to suggest the negative side of personification: its tendency toward sentimentality and reductionism, not to mention cliché. Used without awareness and a certain amount of irony, personification is problematic. Instead of seeing an object or an *other*, we see ourselves and what we want to see.

But personification has deep roots in many cultures and in the human psyche. It goes back to the gods taking the shapes of animals and supplications to the objects and animals that were most crucial to the survival of the tribe. In the Psalms trees clap their hands and hills leap. How much more expansive and expressive that is, compared to the lone psalmist making those gestures.

When I think of a figure like the coyote in Native American culture, I am aware that the trickster figure comes out of deep experience and knowledge of the world. To imagine or inhabit another creature, we must have an intimate awareness of it, must acknowledge it with both respect and humility. We can call this kind of figure naive or primitive, but poetry needs to remember its roots. A poem can't be all control, pure machine. It has to keep itself open to both the primitive and the spiritual.

When used well, personification allows us to place our own psychic dramas outside ourselves and then let them play out. Projection is one way we convey inner thought to the reader.

I think of Louise Glück's talking flowers in *The Wild Iris*, how they become characters who embody what would otherwise be a pretty abstract conversation, and make it vivid, character-driven and memorable. There is Adam Zagajewski's German radio in "Electric Elegy," to which he says, *no one, radio, will accuse you of treason; / no your only sin was obedience...*" In both of these examples, there is a respect for the figure that is speaking. In Glück's case, the poem's speaker isn't addressing the flowers, but they are addressing her. The flower has the wisdom, the upper hand. In Zagajewski's poem, the speaker does address the radio, but it is with affection, with empathy for the radio's position, and clearly we understand the radio is a stand-in for a whole culture.

Personification works when the poem makes clear that the writer knows perfectly well what she or he is doing and does not intend to define the object itself—that easily could become reductive—but rather to let the object define or elucidate something in the human world.

Empathy is another element that can be developed through personification. When Dickinson speaks of *nature's people* she doesn't make them cute, but rather suggests the bond she feels with them. And through the process of close observation and respect, that *narrow fellow in the grass* becomes utterly other by the poem's end. Personification also can be used to redress cultural marginalization as in the case of Edward Hirsch speaking as a buzzard in "Apologia for Buzzards":

> Nobody welcomes me, nobody. And yet
> the sun that beats through the ribs of the sky
> beats with a heavy pulse, like the heart,
> hollowing out the skull and spoiling the flesh.

To use personification well, a writer has to respect the object or creature being observed, and make it clear that there is a distance between the actual object and the use to which it is being put. We have to acknowledge the limits of empathy and understanding. That is where the irony comes in. When Larry Levis has one of the trees in his poem "The Two Trees" remind the speaker, *You do not even / Have a car anymore*, we understand that as psychic drama, perhaps the speaker poking fun at his own self-pity, even as he tries to take solace in the trees. It's a moment of subtle and mixed emotion—shame, sadness, and also humor.

Personification isn't something to just toss into a poem—give the tree a thought to surprise the reader. It is most effective when the poet intends from the start to play with the figures. Think of Laura Jensen's "Bad Boats" opening with *They are like women because they sway./ They are like men because they swagger.*

Personification often works best when there is an element of humor—*Geez, I'm talking to a tree*—or even an element of extravagance—*Yes, I'm describing boats in terms of gender, and I'm not stopping there.* As with other uses of persona, the mask can allow a writer to speak more freely than she ever would in her own voice. It can create the psychic distance that makes the poem expansive rather than focused on the poet's self. It can embody empathy and redress marginalization. It can be just plain fun.

One way to play with personification is to create a relationship between two objects, say one manufactured and one natural. How do they relate? What emotional dynamics exist? Who desires what? Who resists? It is, of course, ourselves we are watching play out in this dynamic. But the point is, we are watching, not abstracting, not lecturing, and it is something dynamic that's being played out. Dynamic. Play.

Poem and Prompt

Downhearted

Six horses died in a tractor-trailer fire.
There. That's the hard part. I wanted
to tell you straight away so we could
grieve together. So many sad things,
that's just one on a long recent list
that loops and elongates in the chest,
in the diaphragm, in the alveoli. What
is it they say, heart-sick or downhearted?
I picture a heart lying down on the floor
of the torso, pulling up the blankets
over its head, thinking this pain will
go on forever (even though it won't).
The heart is watching Lifetime movies
and wishing, and missing all the good
parts of her that she has forgotten.
The heart is so tired of beating
herself up, she wants to stop it still,
but also she wants the blood to return,
wants to bring in the thrill and wind of the ride,
the fast pull of life driving underneath her.
What the heart wants? The heart wants
her horses back.

—Ada Limón

Limón takes an incident from the news—the death of six horses—and uses it as the jumping-off point for her poem. She then moves from the news story to the chest to the heart.

The poet takes an imaginative leap as she personifies the heart. It is female, suffers emotionally, and watches movies on TV. Notice how the poet uses imagery to facilitate the personification: *I picture a heart lying down on the floor."* This heart wants grief to stop, a grief that feels like being pulled by horses. By the end of the poem, the poet skillfully circles back to the beginning of the poem. The ending comes as a surprise, yet it is a perfectly logical ending point.

Notice that the poet speaks in a casual voice and employs direct address. She mixes somewhat technical diction—chest, diaphragm, alveoli—with casual everyday diction. This mixture adds to the tone of the poem as do the questions (e.g., the speaker's confusion over the correct word: *What / is it they say, heart-sick or downhearted?*) and the one parenthetical insertion.

Notice also the poet's use of anaphora as she repeats "The heart" at the beginning of three sentences. She also repeats *wants* five times in the last six lines. These repetitions give emphasis to what the heart wants and add music to the poem.

Finally, notice how Limón weaves a constellation of sound-alike words throughout the poem: *hard, heart, head, parts, wants, wind, what.* The result is sonic unity and a subtle kind of music.

✐ ✐ ✐

Before you begin your own poem, scour today's news for a story about some kind of disaster. Keep it local rather than global. Announce the news as you begin your draft. Ramble a bit, as if you were chatting with a pal.

Find some kind of connection between your disaster and a part of the body. As logically as possible, make the leap to that body part.

Personify the body part in such a way that it expresses emotion.

Pay attention to voice and tone. Use direct address. Mix casual diction with more technical words. Ask a few questions.

Use some anaphora.

Use a circular structure, returning at the end to the beginning.

Have a knockout closing line. Don't quit until you've got a line that surprises you.

Try threading a series of sound-alike words throughout the poem. Choose a dominant word as the anchor sound—for example, *flesh* might be followed by *flash, flair, mesh, amass, mess, caress.*

Sample Poems

Tornado in Manzanita

They're saying on TV that a freak
tornado took down a third
of the trees in this town.
Friends in the city are calling
to make sure we're ok. I guess
I should have let someone know,
but what's there to say? I can't
describe sorrow or the fragrance
of cedar on wet winter mornings.
I don't know how to grieve.
Out on the street, the shock
of debris, cottages stripped
of shingles, massive old hemlocks
twisted and split. I feel my lungs
open and close with their hungers,
my breath rising and falling like heavy
wings. More like a body inside
my body, breathing me. Body
of sadness, of work and repair, body
of panic and prayer and ravenous
want. It's pointless to look out
the window for comfort now,
with all the branches gone.

—Emily Ransdell

Bright Blue

A two-year-old girl drowned in a neighbor's pool,
the paper reports. Tottered across the road
while Mom was painting her nails at the table.
Broad daylight, cars passing, barefoot toddler.
Is it the mom's fault? an old friend asks on the phone.
I think: isn't it always. The child, in love
with bright blue things, the sky, the water,
must have dipped a toe, said the mother, lost
her balance, toppled in. A toe. The big toe, no doubt,
the hallux. Don't tell me that child's other bones
didn't thirst for it, too. I raised three daughters
in Idaho after their father split for Cancun,
taking his halluxes with him, his metatarsals.
Big man toe tapping on the kitchen floor as he told me,
man toe ugly as sin. My friend, that girl didn't teeter.
She jumped, mad at her mother for not painting
her toes, the big toes, oh, and can't you just feel
the terrible two of them crossing the plane
of that magic water?

—Jenny Hubbard

Craft Tip #21: Divine is Mine: Poetry's Reckless Declarations

—Diane Seuss

In poetry, all bets are off. You don't have to be heroic, and it's probably best if you're not. You needn't be good, or wise, or holy. In fact, the best poems about holiness are the ones which involve wrestling (Hopkins) or being ravished (Donne). Likewise, in poetry it is probably more interesting to be unreasonable than reasonable, to practice injudiciousness rather than diplomacy, to perform assertion rather than to hem and haw, to declare rather than suggest. Whitman doesn't recommend you join him in his self-celebration; he demands it: *And what I assume you shall assume, / For every atom belonging to me as good belongs to you.* Not only will you share his assumptions, you'll share his atoms. This claim is audacious and authoritative. Through the fifty-two sections of "Song of Myself," Whitman *owns* you.

Where Whitman sprawls, colonizing both the page and you, Dickinson digs a deep but narrow well: *Area—no test of depth*, she writes in a letter. Her assertions are lean but emphatic. She doesn't *suggest* that maybe the brain is wider than the sky, she declares it, and not only is it wider than the sky, it is *just the weight of God*, a heretic moment if there ever was one, especially from the pen of a woman in nineteenth-century America. Let's take a mini-tour of some of her first lines: *Much Madness is divinest Sense—to a discerning Eye—; This World is not Conclusion, Beauty—be not caused—It is; The Bible is an antique Volume, Renunciation—is a piercing Virtue;* and *After great pain, a formal feeling comes.* There is also the assertive imperative: *Tell all the Truth but tell it slant*, and the cheeky claim: *Title divine is mine.* Dickinson's poems, it has been said, begin where other poems end. *Beauty—be not caused—It is* sounds like a final flourish and not an opening gambit. Where does one go, from a Dickinson first line declaration, but into uncharted territory?

In my own work, I sometimes use declaration, frontloaded into the titles of poems, on subjects with which I feel most shaky.

Beauty is over, for instance. *Either everything is sexual or nothing is.* These declarations are performed with a surety I rarely feel in life. In a sense, I set myself up to have to follow a claim like a voracious dog whose leash I must hang onto for dear life. It is not a useless exercise to stick an anemic poem on a wooden chair under a bare light bulb and demand of it: What is your thesis and where is your evidence? It is often true that the best thesis is nearly ludicrous, almost impossible to prove. That way invention and madness lie.

I can think of no more crucial use of this approach than William Carlos Williams' *so much depends upon* in his poem "The Red Wheelbarrow." Imagine the poem without that rhetorical strategy. There would only be a scattering of objects, witnessed and transmitted to the page. He raises the stakes with those four words—*so much depends upon*—that frame the scene as wrenchingly and mysteriously essential, a declaration rather than a description.

Fast forward to now, and Fatimah Asghar's "Pluto Shits on the Universe," whose opening lines proclaim, *Today, I broke your solar system. Oops. / My bad.* Like Whitman, like Dickinson in her way, Asghar is performing a version of the self via the marginalized planet Pluto that is undoubtedly less nuanced than the self she walks around with. There is grandiosity, a flamboyance that is thrilling in its *lack* of dimensionality, its full-frontal attack: *Your year? Your year ain't / shit but a day to me.*

When a poet is willing to forcefully proclaim, all hell breaks loose. In the artifice of a less dimensional self, there is theater, archetype. There are systemic realignments. Words lose their practiced banality and are brandished with a potency that is political, transformative. Chaos is un-nouned, becomes kinetic, a verb that affirms the cosmic power of the marginalized self. Could it be that declaration is a crucial mode for those who, in one way or another, are exiled? Let me put it another way: Declaration is a crucial mode for those who are exiled.

Poem and Prompt

The Day

We walked at the edge of the sea, the dog,
still young then, running ahead of us.

Few people. Gulls. A flock of pelicans
circled beyond the swells, then closed
their wings and dropped head-long
into the dazzle of light and sea. You clapped
your hands; the day grew brilliant.

Later we sat at a small table
with wine and food that tasted of the sea.

A perfect day, we said to one another,
so that even when the day ended
and the lights of houses among the hills
came on like a scattering of embers,
we watched it leave without regret.

That night, easing myself toward sleep,
I thought how blindly we stumble ahead
with such hope, a light flares briefly—Ah, Happiness!
then we turn and go on our way again.

But happiness, too, goes on its way,
and years from where we were, I lie awake
in the dark and suddenly it returns—
that day by the sea, that happiness,

though it is not the same happiness,
not the same darkness.

—Peter Everwine

Everwine takes on the difficult job of defining happiness, an abstract concept. To do that, he selects a single day that was filled with happiness, a day he characterizes as *perfect*, and describes it with lots of concrete details. He begins by setting the scene—the sea, two people, a dog. Notice the descriptive details in stanza 2—the gulls, the pelicans circling beyond the swells, the closing of their wings as they *dropped head-long / into the dazzle of light and sea*. The scene is full of visual imagery. Note, especially, the light image, *the dazzle of light and sea*, which is later contrasted with dark images.

The day progresses in chronological order with the couple moving in stanza 3 to a table somewhere else. Imagery continues, but now it's the sense of taste that the poet appeals to as the couple enjoyed *wine and food that tasted of the sea*.

The poet does something interesting with point of view. Initially, he uses first person plural *We*, but, in stanza 5, he shifts to first person singular point of view as the speaker recalls having mused philosophically while in bed: *I thought how blindly we stumble ahead / with such hope, a light flares briefly—Ah, Happiness!* Notice that this shift in point of view is accompanied by a shift in time from the past to the present. The speaker is once again awake *in the dark*, recalling that special day and again feeling the happiness he felt back then. These shifts allow us to infer that the happiness did not last.

✐ ✐ ✐

Let's take on the challenge of defining and capturing happiness, a task that has been undertaken by other poets such as Jane Kenyon and Raymond Carver, both of whom wrote poems entitled "Happiness." Let's try the method used by Everwine.

Choose a single day from the past, one that in retrospect seems perfect, or at least part of the day does.

Include yourself and one other person in a particular setting. Proceed from the beginning of the experience to the end of it, pinpointing the highlights of the day. Use descriptive details, but keep them simple, uncomplicated.

Begin your draft in first person plural. Begin in the past with past tense. Later, around the midway point, shift to first person singular. As you shift the point of view, also shift time and tense to the present.

Include a contrasting pair of images, e.g., fire and water, hot and cold, quiet and loud, sweet and sour.

Sample Poems

A Walk in the Park

We parked our car, tugged tight at baseball caps
to block the sun, and set off
through lush Brackenridge Park,
sheltered
by shady oaks,
birdsong abundant as air,
soft babble at narrow river's bend.

In unison we stepped, kicked
a loose stone down dappled path,
laughed
and wended toward our best-loved bench
to watch a lonesome noon-bleached heron pause
on one leg, cautious, in the spillway.

Afterward, we lunched at home
on summer's bounty: peppers, yellow and red,
leafy greens, a healthy grain-packed bread,
cups of Jasmine tea
and pieces of dark chocolate.

Later, we flopped into our bed—
exhaustion
from a day of grace. You said:
Tomorrow, let's do it again.

Tonight in bed, I bless my tired legs,
recall our steps, each promise made that day,
each secret shared,
alert
to rise and fall of your unhurried breath.

Once, under dimming skies, I went ahead.
A hitch in your left leg slowed down your pace.
Go at your own speed, you said. *I'll catch up.*
And I did, walked in
silence,
suddenly afraid
to turn lest you be gone.

—Linda Simone

Dispatch from the Middle Distance

Having survived the wreckage of two marriages,
we arrive at this late morning in middle age

bright-eyed and intact. Alive and needing
nothing, we laze the wide, white beach of my bed—

this island of found hours—our words
more careful than our mouths. In the silence

of the empty house, we don't speak
of our children's grief, of the ways we weren't

enough for our spouses but would have stayed
anyway. We see how we've been freed by debris.

Here, in the quiet of the workday, your face—
a marvel of lived-life and laugh-lines—

hangs for limitless minutes in the air above me.
I trace the cherry blossoms inked on your forearm

and a smile blooms between us; I close my eyes
as the sympathetic sun breaks from behind clouds.

Someday—later, we will speak of it—we will travel
to Japan, where we can wander through petal-light

and the silence of combed stones, together
in a country where the beauty in brokenness

isn't just an idea, but a bowl mended with gold
we can hold in our hands and lift to our lips.

—Megan Gannon
published in *Crazyhorse*

Top Tips: Sixteen Tips, Quips, and Pontifications

—Robert Wrigley

1. A poem is rarely a performance by a solo instrument; it is most often three: syntax, which is the bass; consonants, which are percussion; and vowels, which are the notes of its melody.

2. Pound: *The poem fails when it strays too far from the song. The song fails when it strays too far from the dance.* That this should be both inarguably true and total nonsense is fascinating to me.

3. Dote upon the long vowel.

4. Always live alliteratively.

5. Count syllables, if only for the hell of it. A decasyllabic line will often require continual retooling (stitching and unstitching, even), if the right margin is to matter.

6. The right margin must matter.

7. If you do not know what comes next, imagine two possibilities: pulling something down from what's already there, or lighting out for the territories. This latter is what Richard Hugo called *writing off the subject.* The point, however, is to make the latter the former.

8. Anything that increases the degree of difficulty in the poem's making is to be sought out.

9. Dylan Thomas: *[A poem] is the rhythmic, inevitably narrative, movement from an over-clothed blindness to a naked vision.*

10. A pair of Larkin's slanted-unto-horizontalness rhymes in "High Windows": *kids* and *diaphragm,* and *lives* and *harvester.* Brilliant as well as enviable. Just as dazzling is the meter of the A-rhyme phrasings of stanza 4: *of the priest. He* and *And immediately.*

11. There are prose poems I love, but I don't understand the impulse to write them. I depend on the line. I thrive on its incremental tensions. I aspire for almost every line a life of its own, a statement within the poem or its syntax that enlarges, or disrupts, seamlessly. I am not opposed to prose poems; I do not hate them, as my students have accused me. I'm just not interested in writing them. Poems, yes. Prose, sure.

12. The most useful sound at or near the end of a line is one that shall be sounded again, in the first half of the subsequent line: a method of allowing sound to drive the poem, rather than the poet.

13. Having something to say is a curse; having an ax to grind is deadly. But everything makes poetry happen.

14. A poem is a rhetorical device. It persuades. It is an argument on its own behalf. (Forster: *Information points to something else. A poem points to nothing but itself.*)

15. Nothing is ever worn out, used up.

16. There are no rules. Learn them all.

Bonus Prompt: The Mood Poem

This is a variation of John Gardiner's exercise for fiction writers. It is equally useful for poets.

Picture in your head a particular building, e.g., the Empire State Building, the Guggenheim Museum, the Pentagon, or something local such as a nearby church, factory, or department store.

Now describe the building through the eyes of someone who is unhappy. Do not let the speaker say that she is unhappy or tell what has or hasn't happened to cause the unhappiness.

Once you have a draft, create a title that hints at the cause of the unhappiness, e.g., "Missing Him," "After the Funeral," or "The Divorce."

Now describe the same building from the perspective of someone who is happy. Again, don't let the speaker say he is happy, but let your title set the mood and direction for the poem.

This exercise should demonstrate not only the importance of images but also the importance of titles.

Another experiment for you to try: Switch from first to third person point of view.

On a different day, try this activity with a body of water, a garden, a fence, or a train station.

VIII. Transforming Your Poems

*Poetry is the impish attempt to paint
the color of the wind.*

—Maxwell Bodenheim

Craft Tip #22: Point of View: Who's Talking Now?

—Sharon Bryan

No one is surprised to hear fiction writers talk about point of view, but I find it even more interesting and illuminating to look at point of view in poems: Where is this being seen from? What voice is speaking? Each point of view has very different effects and its own advantages and problems to solve.

1. First person singular, *I*, is the most common point of view in contemporary poetry, and might be a speaker who seems to have a lot in common with the poet, or it might be a very different persona or mask, another identity. An *I* poem is seen and heard through one character, so it's usually easy to recognize the tone and emotions, but it's limited to what that speaker knows and thinks as in Sylvia Plath's "The Arrival of the Bee Box": *I ordered this, this clean wood box, / Square as a chair and almost too heavy to lift.* Only the speaker can know and tell about the box; the reader sees the box through the speaker's eyes.

2. First person plural, *we*, can mean anything from *we two* to *we humans*. It's not used often, but appears in one of the best known contemporary poems, "We Real Cool," by Gwendolyn Brooks: *We real cool. We / Left school.* Here, the *we* speaks for and as a group, a group of young pool players. Readers can safely assume that these pool players have similar lives, share the same experiences in the same way, and share the same perceptions about their lives.

3. Second person, *you*, is incredibly elastic. It can be addressed to one other person or to a group, or it can even be used as an informal *one*. Speaking to an intimate *you* might lapse into language too private to follow. Marvin Bell doesn't let that happen in "To Dorothy": *You are not beautiful, exactly. / You are beautiful inexactly.* The title makes it clear that the *you* is a woman named Dorothy. The reader has the pleasure of eavesdropping on a private conversation.

When the *you* isn't directed at one person, the pronoun's antecedent can be unclear as in Richard Hugo's "Degrees of Gray in Philipsburg": *You might come here some day on a whim. / Say your life broke down.* Here we see how flexible *you* can be. Hugo's *you* could be just anyone, a general *you*.

4. Third person, *he* or *she*, has the advantage of focus plus the distance of an external narrator. Adrienne Rich's "Living in Sin" uses third person *she* in a way that gives us both distance and closeness: *She had thought the studio would keep itself; / no dust upon the furniture of love.* The reader knows what the woman had thought and can infer that she was disappointed, that love did not live up to her expectation. Rich, because of the limitations of the external third person, engages images that do a lot towards revealing feelings.

The easiest way to get at the effects of point of view, in your poems or someone else's, is to do some rewriting.

Robert Frost's "Stopping by Woods on a Snowy Evening" begins, *Whose woods these are I think I know*. Compare that to *Whose woods these are he thinks he knows*. For this poem, third person would have been the wrong choice.

Look again at Gwendolyn Brooks's "We Real Cool": *We real cool. We / Left school.* Consider what would have been lost if Brooks had decided to use the more personal singular first person: *I real cool,* or the distanced second person of *You real cool*, or the singular third person of *He real cool*, or the collective plural third person of *They real cool*.

Consider Adrienne Rich's third person in "Living in Sin": *She had thought the studio would keep itself; / no dust upon the furniture of love*. Now change that to first person: *I had thought the studio would keep itself*. Then try third person plural: *They had thought the studio would keep itself*. Does the poem work at all in a different point of view?

Each of these revisions creates a different poem. Nothing opens up a poem you're working on more than revising it, seeing it new, from a different point of view.

Poem and Prompt

Baby on a Train

Wartime, the Santa Fe Chief
shudders out of Los Angeles
crammed with demobbed soldiers,
a green wave sweeping home
after V Day.
My mother negotiates the aisle
with me on her hip, absent my father,
her caramel colored tweed suitcase
passed along by the soldiers
until she finds her seat,
the sole civilian in the car.
Emerging from the tunnel at Cajon Pass,
we begin our braked decline into Victorville,
the mirage that is the Mojave.
The soldier opposite my mother
introduces himself, asking politely
if he may hold me. She hands me over,
soon airborne over uplifted faces of soldier
after soldier, who have not seen
their children for years, some never.
They pass me reverently overhead,
seat to seat, the length of the rollicking train
and back again—
men who survived Anzio,
Normandy and The Bulge,
inhaling my scent, their unshaved
chins rubbing my scalp,
trigger fingers tickling my feet,
arms rocking me, a company of arms.

—Roger Camp

In this seemingly simple narrative, Camp tells a story of when he was a baby. But what's unusual is that he doesn't tell the story as if it's one he heard and is now retelling as an adult; instead, he uses first person point of view and present tense, writing as if the speaker is now a baby. Of course, babies don't tell stories, so this is an impressive imaginative feat.

Characteristic of a narrative poem, we get setting, time, characters, and action. The speaker is on a train traveling through California after the end of WW II. He is accompanied by his mother and a group of demobilized soldiers. One soldier asks to hold the speaker. That soldier then passes the baby overhead so that all the soldiers, men who have missed their own children, can enjoy the baby. The action is so simple, yet so tender.

Camp provides some details. We have a list of places that are part of the setting. We have a list of the battles the soldiers fought in. We know the color of the mother's suitcase. We know that the soldiers tickle the baby's feet. Most intriguing, however, is what we do not know. So much more is said in the poem because of what the poet leaves out. There's mystery. Why is the mother traveling alone? Where is the absent father? Why isn't he here? No names are given to any of the characters, but their gestures convey a lot, e.g., the unshaved chins of the soldiers rubbing the baby's scalp, the tickling of the baby's feet, the arms rocking the baby. Notice that these gestures involve parts of the body.

Notice, too, the poet's diction, how apt and metaphorical it is: the soldiers are a *green wave sweeping home*, the baby is *airborne over the uplifted faces of soldier / after soldier*, the men have *trigger fingers*. Notice, particularly, the closing line's image: *arms rocking me, a company of arms*. These men after years at war have put down the other kind of arms.

You're going to write a baby poem. You might begin by looking through some old photos of you as a baby or by recalling a baby story told to you by a relative. Get an event/action in mind, e.g., your baptism, first trip to the zoo, first time being left with a babysitter, being licked by a dog, being nursed or bathed.

Choose a location. Make a list of setting details. Include names of the parts of your setting.

Now begin your draft. Introduce your time and location right away. Jump right in. Freewrite about what happens. Use first person point of view speaking as the baby (but, please, no baby talk). Use present tense as if the action is happening now. Include as much detail as you feel inclined to use.

Weave in the setting details from your list.

As you revise, pare down the details. Keep the narrative simple: this will be a less-is-more kind of poem.

Pay attention to your diction. Make it relevant to the narrative. Let it rise to metaphor.

Sample Poems

Childhood

So I push her off the swing,
step over her in the scooped-out grass
of our new backyard in Camp Hill,
Pennsylvania, and climb on.
Our mother rushes to scoop her up.
Our father keeps filming as the swing
rocks once, twice, then our mother
grabs me by the arm. I'm three,
my sister's one, they've dressed us
in seersucker playsuits, blue for her
and red for me, and skinned our hair
back with sparkly barrettes. We're
newly here from Wetzlar, where
the Nazi major laced the garden
of our requisitioned house
with razor blades, and I came in
the kitchen one day, arms dripping blood—
back to the States on the Army ship,
where they leashed me to a halter
to stop me falling overboard.
Our dad has been taking home movies,
how cute, the plan was, big sister
pushing little sister, how they love
each other. But I just want to swing.

—Ann Fisher-Wirth

Ablution

It's early evening, past dinner
in the East End flat. My mother
draws my bath in the kitchen sink.
Heat radiates off the shingled siding
of the house next door, close enough
to hit with a stone, but there's a river
breeze as well through the tall
double windows my mother swung open
to encourage some air. I'm waiting
in my high chair, naked chest already
wiped clean of strained beef and applesauce.
What's coming is one of my favorite things.
I beat happily on the metal tray
when my mother bends toward me
to lift me up in her cool, sure arms.
I gaze over her shoulder at the yellow kitchen
as she cradles me, removing my plastic pants
and diaper with a practiced hand. Then
she lowers me into my private basin,
tepid enough to bar a chill yet refreshing.
She saturates a cloth and squeezes rivulets
over my back and belly as I converse
with the lights playing off the ripples
I slap and splash. My mother finishes
with a baptism over my nearly bald scalp,
making sure the drips don't blind me as I
take in everything I love: the reflecting pool
in my lap, the breath of summer through the screen,
the tickle of droplets running down my neck, and
my mother most of all, her generous arms full of towel.
Next she'll dry me, oil me, and powder me
until I smell like the tea roses
near the backyard wall where the trains chug by.

—Nancy Susanna Breen

Craft Tip #23: The (Perpetual) Metamorphosis

—Jennifer Givhan

Get magical real. Get fabulist and strange. Start transforming: your images, your narratives, your speaker (your *self*). In my drafts I tend to write the same beating heart over and over. Cheryl Strayed calls it the *second heart* and writes about getting down on the floor to pull this second heart from one's chest onto the page. I think of *The Two Fridas,* each with a heart, one broken. Tony Hoagland calls it one's *mythical wound*. In *Real Sofistikashun* he writes:

> A real, diehard, indestructible, irresolvable obsession in a poet is nothing less than a blessing. The poet with an obsession never has to search for subject matter. It is always right there, welling up like an Artesian spring on a piece of property with bad drainage... Emily Dickinson's critics say that death was her *flood subject*, the theme that electrified her language whenever she approached it... The poet without a compelling, half-conscious story of the world may not have a heat source catalytic enough to channel into the work of a lifetime.

Like Hoagland's poet, I don't know that I can command my obsessions, but I have learned how to transfuse them into the lifeblood of my poems, to channel them and transform them on the page so that I'm not writing identical poems one after the other like little broken baby robots down a factory belt (there's an example of my mythical wound—transformed via metaphor).

So here's what you do: Transform your trauma into something magical, marvelous. Give your pubescent self a pair of antlers and see what new angle your poem takes with that small but important change; turn your broken-bodied self into a train station and ride the train of yourself away. Gregor Samsa had to transform into a giant beetle before he could understand the extent of his problems. Frida had to birth herself, for she could birth nothing else living into this world.

In our poems, as in our lives, we have the marvelous ability to transform reality, as well as to see the transformative reality that already exists around and within us. As Jane Hirshfield writes, *Hyperbole, the fabulous, the straight-out lies of metaphor and fabricated image—when the impossible enters the mind, the capacity of experience increases...the impossible enters poems.*

This metamorphosis can take place at any point in the writing process, from drafting to revision. In drafting, it's akin to first thought worst thought. Take that first thought somewhere stranger, wilder, magical. Don't worry about the logical simile-making brain. Go passionately forth into the forests of metaphor. Get lost there. For example, if I were to start writing a poem this very moment, I might be tempted to write of a broken egg. I've written a dozen egg poems! I could fit them into a carton and take them to market to sell; my poor hen-heart will not let up! So I'll go magical instead. The broken egg hatches regardless. My little lost ones wake up. The things I've buried beneath the barnyard start to crow. And grow. And take over the farm.

In revision, I've taken my stalest poems that use my repetitive imagery and by seeing them in a new light, giving those images a twist, I've resuscitated them. Don't give up on your obsessions, your mythic wounds. Instead, see them from a new angle, a new perspective. Same issue. Different light. Go back to those lost poems you've left by the wayside. Find an image or narrative detail or lyrical moment and take it somewhere impossible. And in its impossibility, let it heal the poem. Let it heal you.

Poem and Prompt

Genealogy

One of her parents was a flame, the other a rope.
One was a tire, the other a dial tone.

In the night she'd wake to a hum and the faint
smell of burnt rubber.

One of her parents was a flag, the other a shoe.

The ideogram tattooed on her lower back
is the one for dog-trying-to-run-on-ice.

One of her parents was a star already gone out,
the other a cup she carried into the night,
convinced it was fragile.

One of her parents she drank, the other she dreamed.

In the revolving door of her becoming,
one pushed from inside, one from without.
Thus, her troubled birth, her endless stammer.

One was an eyebrow, the other a wink.
How they amused each other.

One was a candle, the other a bird. She was ashamed
of not burning, embarrassed she couldn't fly.

She was a girl calling across the ice
to a dog she didn't have.

—Betsy Sholl

In this inventive genealogical study, Sholl's third person speaker imagines in metaphors the origins of a girl. The speaker describes each of the girl's parents in a series of non-human items.

Notice the structure of the poem: One of the parents was A; the other was B. This structure prepares us for contrasts. But that's not what we get. Instead, we get unexpected, curious juxtapositions. Each pairing is followed by some kind of statement about the girl which may or may not be a consequence of the previous pairing. In stanza 1, for example, one parent was a flame, the other a dial tone. That is picked up in the following stanza as the girl awakes and hears a hum and smells something burning. However, stanza 3 has one parent as a flag, the other as a shoe. The following stanza, with its description of the girl's ideogram, doesn't seem to bear any connection to what we've just learned about the girl's parents.

Notice how skillfully Sholl balances pattern and unpredictability. Just when we've accepted that we're not going to get opposites, in stanza 7 she gives us opposites: *one parent pushed from inside, one from without.*

Sholl weaves in references to fire (the star already gone out, a candle, the girl's shame over not burning) and to its opposite, ice (the ideogram is the one for dog-trying-to-run-on-ice and the girl in the last stanza is *calling across the ice / to a dog she didn't have*). Thus, Sholl gives the poem some unity.

✎ ✎ ✎

For your own genealogy poem, you might want to also use third person. Or you might want to try first person and consider your own genealogy. You can use parents as Sholl does or you might want to change it up a bit and consider a pairing between brother and sister, son and daughter, cat and dog, first boyfriend and second (or last). Of course, you can make the female character a male.

You might find it helpful to begin with two lists—column A and column B. In column A quickly insert a list of nouns, not considering what will go in column B. When done, do the same in Column B.

Now begin with one item from A and match it up with something in B, but not with what's right next to it.

Follow Sholl's structural plan. Combine some pattern with some unpredictability.

Find an image or image pair from early in the poem and weave in references to it several times later in the poem. This will give the poem some unity via imagery.

This prompt encourages you to take leaps of imagination. Don't thwart it by trying to be overly literal or logical. Be playful. Invite strangeness to enter.

Sample Poems

Lovers

One of her lovers was a library, the other a lawn chair.
One was a vase, the other a dandelion.

One of her lovers was a fledgling, the other a boulder.

The knickknacks on her shelf were named "Lucky" and "Flip,"
lifelike giraffes in playful poses.

One of her lovers was the ocean always returning,
the other a swervy bat devouring gnats.

One of her lovers she floated in, the other she sought out at night.

In the thickening of her love life,
one enveloped her as the crush of rosemary,
one peeled easy like an orange; hence her kaleidoscopic hunger.

One was summer rain, the other tropical sun;
how they both were agreeable.

One was an oak tree, the other white pine. She was an acorn
in the mouth of the squirrel and the pine cone idle on the grass.

She was the elephant stretching her lanky trunk
to the air for good luck.

In the summer she blew wishes and flicked ants
off the peonies.

—Camille Norvaisas

Siblings

Her brother was a snow shovel, she was a pair of Sunday gloves.
She was penny candy, he the family bible.

In their family, it was okay for girls to be frivolous.

He was an encyclopedia of fears, she was the latest fad.
She was a swallowed laugh, he was a mouthful of tears.

Her brother was collectible vinyl, she was 8-track.
She'd wake each morning, humming a song
she could never name.

Her brother was a bicycle collecting dust in the shed,
she was a book read under the covers of night.

She said she'd be happy to be secondhand
silver. He said he wished he was
a stack of rare comic books.

Her brother was a boardwalk carousel,
content with repeated circles. She was a Wild Mouse.

He was the ideogram for Prince, she knew
she was a raspberry beret.
She wanted to be a red Corvette.

Her brother was a glass half full, she the glass half empty.
She was the girl always freshening their drinks.

He was a chance of snow, she was 78 and sunny.
She was the door knocker, he was the door.

In their family, sons were expected to be strong.

She's the girl standing alone at the Victrola,
staring at an empty turntable, spinning and silent.

—Gail Comorat

Craft Tip #24: First Thought, Worst Thought

—Traci Brimhall

I'd like to believe Allen Ginsberg meant well when he said, *First thought, best thought.* I'm sure it's supposed to encourage a fearless mind, a spontaneity that can leap and make strange and startling connections. But for me, my first thought is often my most expected thought; my first drafts can contain familiar images and an embarrassing amount of cliché. However, I don't think that makes those drafts bad or failures. It means I am someone who must revise into strangeness rather than someone who must revise into clarity.

Step one in avoiding my own banality is asking where my fear is in the poem. Fear is usually the emotional impulse of a poem for me, but sometimes I spend the length of the poem running away from it rather than entering into it. Even if it's just a line, a poem—for me—must confront what asked it to write in the first place. Emily Dickinson said, *Nature is a haunted house— but Art—is a house that tries to be haunted.* So I make sure there's a ghost in residence before I move in, or I wait around during full moons with my electromagnetic sensor and a Ouija board, figuratively speaking.

Once my poems are honest enough about their fears, I have to interrogate the language. Ginsberg seems to have been able to let his mind reach an ecstatic place in the moment, but I have a longer practice. I need to concentrate to let go. I find ecstasy in some balance of play and patience.

One way I find new energy for a poem is by finding even five new words for it. This doesn't mean adding five new words but replacing five. I know it seems simple, silly even, but for me, when I find five new words, it often has a way of unlocking what's already there, or shaking off those first words that feel so familiar for something alarming and wonderful and new.

Here are some ways I do that, either all of one or in some combination:

1. Opposite Adjectives: I circle familiar adjective-noun pairings. Instead of looking for a synonym for that adjective, I replace it with its opposite or its near-opposite. Suddenly, the *beating* heart is the *beaten* heart. The *smooth white bones* become the *pocked gray bones* or the *yellow bones gnawed open and the marrow licked clean.*

2. Verb Musical Chairs: I circle flat verbs and then rotate. Sometimes when an action is sitting in a different seat, it energizes the words around it differently. Sometimes this works well even with a simple swap between two verbs. Then, instead of the moon glowing and moths flying, the moths glow and the moon flies. Perhaps these changes don't stick, but it helps the familiar become unfamiliar.

3. Noun Shopping: Frankly, sometimes the objects in my poems are flat boring or they're things I overuse. I keep a box of oddities I hope to use in poems someday, and I pull out one of these at random. Sometimes this makes the gold rim of a bullet the gold skirt of a bullet. Sometimes this invigorates lists and makes apples, oranges, and bananas become apples, oranges, and a jar of manticore teeth.

Sometimes this shake-up leads to usable images and metaphors. And, frankly, sometimes it doesn't, but it courts a little strangeness and energy into the poem at spots where my language felt weak and familiar to me. For those of us whose first thought isn't our best thought, there's perhaps a longer road, but I think that relationship with our drafts can yield their own odd ecstasies.

Poem and Prompt

When Sex Was Kissing

In high school I was somehow able to kiss
for three hours continuously without consummation.
I still remember the underwater feel of the car,
how the windows steamed, the binnacle-glow
of the dash pointing us forward towards the trees,
the jerky light outside of a diver approaching
the wreck, pointing at this window, then that,
the policeman asking if we were okay. Sure
we were! The brake handle of the Renault
stuck up awkwardly between us. She wore
the scarab bracelet I'd given her, a pleated
white shirt with a gold circle pin plausibly said
to symbolize virginity, a green-blue plaid
wrap-around skirt closed by a huge safety pin,
and stockings held by garters. Only her Capezio flats
were shucked to the car floor. Deftly, she parried
my hands wandering under her skirt, her blouse,
while somehow welcoming my embrace.
Such fine diplomacy might have saved Poland!
I remember how each cubic inch of her was
agonizingly delightful, the soft hinges
at the back of her knees, her warm wrists touched
with Wind Song, the clean scent of her bubble-cut.
Every one of my cells awoke.
Finally, I went home bug-eyed, stunned,
half-drowned, and sat hours until dawn,
testicles aching—poor, haunted witnesses.

—Hunt Hawkins

In this delightful poem, Hunt Hawkins describes the pleasure of a good old-fashioned make out session. The speaker goes back to high school days and recreates the scene from memory.

The charming descriptive details set the time period as the '50s or '60s, e.g., the details from the girlfriend's outfit: her scarab bracelet, pleated shirt, and wrap-around skirt. Notice, too, the virginity pin and the huge safety pin—her protective armor. Hawkins brings in olfactory images with the details of the scent of Wind Song on the girl's wrists and the *clean scent of her bubble-cut.*

The poet also employs figurative language to convey his scene. Particularly notable is the exploited metaphor that begins in line 3 with the *underwater feel of the car.* There was steam on the windows and a compass inside the binnacle. The speaker was drowning in desire.

The metaphor continues as a *diver* approached, really a policeman. Notice the touch of humor and the casual diction as the policeman asked the young couple if they were okay. The speaker now asserts, *Sure / we were!*

Notice, too, the well-chosen fencing verb, *parried,* as the girl metaphorically fended off the boy's wandering hands. Metaphor moves to hyperbole, the language of love, as the girl's gentle removal of the speaker's hands is compared to diplomacy: *Such fine diplomacy might have saved Poland!* The exaggeration continues as the speaker recalls how *each cubic inch of her was / agonizingly delightful* and how *Every one of my cells awoke.*

The poet returns to the water imagery as the speaker returned home *half-drowned.* The poem ends with a metaphor that makes us laugh out loud as the speaker's aching testicles are compared to *poor, haunted witnesses.*

✍ ✍ ✍

Let's write a kissing poem. First, go back to the past and recall an important kiss or kisses—the first kiss, a French kiss, an unwanted kiss, a stolen kiss, an illicit kiss, a last kiss, a goodbye kiss, perhaps a metaphorical kiss. Your poem need not recall a warmly positive memory of kissing.

Recreate the scene. Make it clear that your first-person speaker is going back to the past. Use descriptive details to call forth that time: What was the music then or the dance style? What were the clothing styles? Any fragrance from aftershave or perfume? Any local color, e.g., flowers, trees, food?

Be sure to include some metaphors. Try to make one of them an exploited metaphor.

Use some hyperbole. If, however, your scene is not a tender one, hyperbole might not work. Try it and see what happens. If your poem becomes overly dramatic, revise it out.

Tip: If your poem recalls a painful kissing scene, you might find that using third person makes it possible for you to write the poem. In subsequent drafts, the poem might demand first person. Listen to your poem. Use the point of view that best serves the poem.

Sample Poems

Record

Ten years later, I can laugh
at how I started out dreading
the night I got my first French kiss,
laugh, too, at how nervous I was with my date, with myself,
how I didn't trust the chemistry
that crackled and burned between us like a lava flow,
how, when he smiled at me in the restaurant,
I had to stop my neck from swiveling
to make sure there wasn't a better, prettier woman behind me.

But then, when I remember him driving me home,
I stop laughing and my body gets quiet and warm,
just like it did in his car after I made some corny joke
about love at first sight and he pulled into the driveway and said,
"It wasn't love at first sight, but I love you now."

And I remember his glance hot and soft
as a September sun on my face
and how I knew he was telling the truth,
our attraction so palpable not even my favorite
Mariah Carey remix playing on his car stereo
could distract me from it, and how my breath
seemed to get tangled in my lungs,
but it didn't matter because suddenly his mouth
was on my mouth, my soul pulled into the pink suction
of his lips, my nose filled with the musk
and sandalwood scent of his cologne,
my awkwardness slipping away from me
like lingerie liberated in his hands
as he guided my hands to the muscles
beneath his respectable khaki shirt,
his tongue touching my tongue,

licking like a needle on a record,
patiently probing and circling as I licked him back,
my rigid black curves spinning and flaring
into a love song as primal and erotic
as the pulsing between my thighs.

—Shayla Hawkins

The Kiss

He was the Hungarian tailor (shorter than I was
at sixteen), the nails on his pinkies long and pointy
enough to pluck threads, his hair in tall marcelled
waves off his forehead, his shoes with extra thick heels.

He owned a business for big and tall men—
all day, his lips rayed with pins, kneeling
to their hems, embracing their girth
with the measuring tape he wore around his neck.

He was my mother's new boyfriend. I called him
"Uncle Steve," as a Hungarian child should an elder.
She asked him to buy me the wool coat from Ginsberg's
display window, the one we could never afford—

navy-blue, its nap as fine as the school uniform blazer
I wished I could have. He brought it to our house,
when my mother and he knew she was over-timing
at the mill. He brought my coat on a hanger,

in a plastic sheath he might have pulled over
the massive pants and jackets he daily fixed.
He held the coat for me, as he knew how to do,
both my arms slipping easily into the sleeves.

He pulled the shoulders up to fluff, fit them just so.
Then he turned me around, his face too close,
the Old Spice aftershave my father used.
When I complained to my father about what

Uncle Steve did next (how I couldn't stop him),
my father chuckled, explained that I was very pretty,
that I was a woman now.
And he brought my right hand to his lips.

—Susanna Rich

Top Tips: Ten Shortcuts: A Busy-Body's Guide to Writing Poetry

—Oliver de la Paz

I've got three boys, all under the age of 12. Two of my boys have special needs and because they're always keeping me busy my writing time is fairly short. But rather than resent how little time I'm afforded, I've managed to put together a few tips and tricks that have helped keep me on task especially when parental/homestead duties take hold. I'm aware that these may not be for everyone but they've worked wonderfully for me in my hurry.

1. Read what you can when you can and keep a small notebook for one-liners, sentences, and scrap words.

I've intermittently kept a journal that contains scraps of lines, whole lines, or interesting words. I use these frequently when I'm feeling stuck or when I need a catalyst to get a poem started. And by no means do I restrict my reading diet to poetry. I read everything—the local newspaper, national newspapers, celebrity magazines, science journals, novels, essays, and, of course, poetry. I'll even transcribe bits of language from museum pamphlets.

2. Keep it light and fast—15 minutes to an hour tops.

If you've got loads and loads of time, great. But I'm constantly on the run, so this hard and fast rule works for me. When I sit at the computer, I keep my time there as short as possible— especially when trying to maintain a sustained writing routine. I mostly apply this structure to my writing time during the summer when I write every day. This strictly applies to newer work/generative work.

3. Revise first.

I go over poems that I've written the previous day to check my gut and determine whether I was in the right frame of mind when I wrote the previous day's draft. It's also a good way for me to get my mind refocused on the act of writing without feeling overwhelmed by white space.

4. Write in dialogue with another piece.

Again, in keeping with the idea that it's often more difficult to write a poem *from scratch*, I like to think of the next poem I'm writing as in conversation with a poem I had previously written. Sometimes those conversations are harsh and take a different tonal direction. Sometimes those conversations are supportive.

5. Use the Pomodoro App.

The Pomodoro Technique is a time-management tool that also structures in breaks. I downloaded an app from the iTunes store and there are versions of the app available on Android phones as well as free software for PCs and Macs. Basically the technique parses out 25-minute increments of productive time and then 5-minute breaks. If you're like me and highly distracted, this is a great tool to maintain focus on writing while also allowing for small diversions here and there.

6. Use your titles as prompts.

I often give myself exercises where I try to reconcile disparate elements into poems. In my third collection, *Requiem for the Orchard*, there are a number of Self-Portrait poems. Often, the Self-Portrait has an angle, for example, I wrote a poem entitled "Self-Portrait in My Mother's Shoes" and another entitled "Self-Portrait with Schlitz, a Pick-Up, and the Snake River." By listing elements in the title, I have to implement those elements somehow in the poem and usually what happens is I'm forced to think about narrative as the connective tissue.

7. Vary your industry.

First off, let's stop thinking about the word *project* pejoratively. Project-centered creation is a mode of producing art that inherently emphasizes an artist's intention. In project-centered work, the decision-making becomes streamlined for the purpose of the greater project. I wholeheartedly believe in intention and in intentionality when it comes to creating art and so this method of writing has been greatly effective for my body of work that has been often characterized as serialized or obsessive. That said, sometimes you need a break from a project. That's why I tend to juggle multiple projects (usually three) at a time. I inevitably get stuck at some juncture in a project so it's always useful to have another writing project at hand.

8. Accept a line as a productive day.

Sometimes you have to for self-care.

9. De-clutter and send that stuff out.

Some of my students envision publishing individual poems as the goal. I see submitting work to journals, magazines, and periodicals as a necessary part of the writing, editing, and revising process. When I come to a juncture where I feel my judgment of my work can progress no further, that's when I send work to journals. And it's not just to get the work published, but it's also to clear my headspace—if the work is out I don't look at it again until it's either accepted or rejected.

10. Think of revision as generative.

I mentioned that I often start my writing activities with revision and I want to go into a bit more specifics about my revision philosophy. I believe that revision is *re-envisioning* a work which often moves a poem beyond its particular shell. Sometimes as part of my revision process I'll attempt to write the tonal opposite of the poem in question. Other times I'll think about the poem that occurred before or after the initiating poem. If you think about revision in this light you'll be able to dream up a number of new poetic scenarios based on an original.

Bonus Prompt: The Make It New Poem

Take a title from an earlier well-known poem. Then write a contemporary poem stimulated by the title. George Bilgere borrowed the title of Christopher Marlow's "The Passionate Shepherd to His Love," a sixteenth-century poem, and then wrote "The Fairly Passionate Shepherd to His Love."

Here are some titles to consider:

> The Flea (John Donne)
> The Unknown Citizen (W. H. Auden)
> Nothing Gold Can Stay (Robert Frost)
> To the Virgins, to Make Much of Time (Robert Herrick)
> I knew a woman (Theodore Roethke)
> Sailing to Byzantium (W. B. Yeats)
> I Sing the Body Electric (Walt Whitman)

You may use a format similar to that of the original or you may come up with your own format. Your poem may or may not incorporate elements of the earlier poem. Bilgere borrows Marlow's famous opening line, *Come live with me and be my love,* but he makes a small addition: *Come live with me and be my unconditional love.* This enhanced line begins his poem and then is repeated as the final line. In between, the poem does its own thing.

IX. Rethinking and Revising

*...the process of revising a poem is no arbitrary
tinkering, but a continued honing of the self
at the deepest level.*

—Jane Hirshfield

Craft Tip #25: Life in the Salt Mines: A Revision Strategy

—Campbell McGrath

Poetry is an inward and intuitive art form, especially that originating gift, the mystery of inspiration, a magical word-hoard, or painted cavern, or breath of the gods from whence poems emerge. Which is just fine and dandy, because who doesn't like opening birthday presents or listening to sweet nothings from the cosmos? But the real work of the poet is revision, a task for which it is wise to adopt a more workmanlike persona. Revision is the salt mine to which, pick in hand, we must all descend in time, the day job that keeps a roof over our metaphorical heads.

For this work—reshaping and unclogging and fine-tuning a poem—it is better to act like an engineer, or a plumber, or even an accountant, than a sleepy-eyed dreamer wandering through the garden waiting for poems to pop out of the roses. So here is a tough-love exercise that might help you move the poem to the next stage. Tools are required, as for any physical trade, in this instance two highlighters of different colors, let's say green and yellow, as well as a solid draft of a poem on which to practice our technique.

Step one is to read through your poem, doing your best to view it as something utterly alien to you—perhaps a biology textbook, or a history of the Crimean War, or a poem translated from ancient Chinese. (Learning to read objectively, divorcing yourself from your own text, is best achieved through endless, cold-blooded practice.)

As you read, use the green highlighter to mark anything that seems *really good*—a strong verb, a well-hewn line, a striking image or a sudden emotional leap. But be tough on the poem, demand excellence, question everything. Is that phrase really as good as it seemed when you wrote it? Is the use of alliteration charming or heavy-handed? Only give the green light to what seems best in the poem.

Now read though the poem again, using the yellow highlighter to mark things that are not, perhaps, extraordinary in themselves, but feel essential to the poem: if it operates like an essay or a meditation there might be a few unmusical lines vital to its argument; if it contains a narrative, some exposition might be justifiable, lines that might otherwise feel flat or prosy. Again, be strict with your approval, but allow the poem a little room to breathe.

At the end of this second pass, consider how much of your poem falls into each of the three categories, green, yellow, and unmarked. (If you are a bit overly-deterministic, as I am, you might want to get a red highlighter and use it on these bypassed passages—but for current purposes let's consider them merely uncolorized.) If you have highlighted only a few isolated words, you might be dealing with a poem that needs more than revision, a poem that should to be taken back to its origin and thoroughly *re-envisioned*. On the other hand, if you have marked almost everything, then you have either written a nearly perfect poem, or you are being a bit too easy on yourself.

There are many possible outcomes, but the expectation is that you will have a poem with substantial representation in all three categories. Depending on how far along the poem is, you might have about a third in each, or perhaps there is a dominant yellow tone, with a few sections in green and the rest unmarked. Even if your text contains only a single uncolorized line, however, you still need to ask yourself a big question— what is it doing in your poem? Why does your poem contain even a single word unworthy of a green or yellow highlight? If you, the author, cannot find anything extraordinary or essential in it, it should not be there. Cut it. Cross it out. Erase the poem down to its green core and rebuild it from there.

Coleridge famously defined poetry as *the best words in the best order*, and even if we fall short of his scrupulousness, we need to acknowledge the rigor and seriousness of purpose he advocates. For Coleridge, the poet's task is to consider every possible way of saying what she wants to say, every syntactical variant, every rhetorical approach, until she has identified the absolute best order. The poet must pick up every word and scrutinize it, like a butterfly behind a magnifying glass, and only put it back on the page when certain it is the best of all possible words. It's a daunting prospect, but also invigorating, even exhilarating, if you love language and making beautiful things.

Even the most inspired poem requires draft upon draft before it can become the best possible version of itself. That's what revision is for—fixing the inevitable imperfections in what we write. So put on your hard hat, find yourself a magnifying glass, grab a pickax—or forego the metaphors. Just take up your highlighters and get to work.

Poem and Prompt

Repairs

Who's kept track of the broken
things you've fixed over the years
repairs you've made as if they were nothing
never doubting you can figure out
what tools to use what steps to take

why leave a task to someone else
when you can do it or at least
you'll try poring over diagrams
squinting at instructions
driving to the hardware store

twice on a Saturday to gather supplies
brackets for the rattling pipes
copper wire solder spackle
hinges slide-lock thermostat
and items I can't even name

no system in this house
seems alien to you no failure
alarming so why am I surprised
that I've learned next to nothing
understood next to nothing

about heat and light and water
relying on you
to know what's wrong
and find a way to fix it
relying on you never to break

—Jody Bolz

Lots of love poems have been written, but this one distinguishes itself by the unusual metaphor which structures it. The poem begins with a direct address to *you*, the beloved. This creates a tone of intimacy, a tone that is nicely at odds with the homely tools and repairs metaphor. The beloved is handy; he fixes things around the house, the way he mends the speaker and their relationship.

Bolz uses several interesting techniques. For one, she employs lists, e.g., in stanza 2 we have the beloved *poring over diagrams / squinting at instructions / driving to the hardware store*. Stanza 3 includes a list of hardware supplies.

Another strategy is the use of parallel phrasing, e.g., line 5 of stanza 1 pairs up *what tools to use* with *what steps to take*. In stanza 4 *no system in this house* pairs up with *no failure alarming*. In stanza 5 we have line 2's *relying on you* repeated in the last line.

Notice also the use of negatives. That's interesting in a poem that's such a positive depiction of love. Stanza 1 has *nothing* and *never*. Stanza 3 has *can't* and stanza 4 repeats *no* and then *next to nothing*.

Finally, notice the absence of punctuation in this poem. No terminal marks, no interior ones. Everything just flows together. Again, we have a nice contrast, this time between the abandonment of punctuation and the formality and orderliness of the stanza format: five 5-line stanzas.

✐ ✐ ✐

For your own love poem, zero in on a single talent your beloved (real or imagined) has. It might be fishing, cleaning, sewing, cooking, or gardening. Compile a list of words/terms that relate to the talent. Describe his/her love and your relationship using those words and terms. Watch the metaphor grow and grow.

Try your hand at some of Bolz's techniques. Pile in some compounds, some negatives, some lists. This will create a sense of abundance.

As you move through several drafts, consider the form for your poem. Try to abandon punctuation. If you can't bear to have everything running together, you might try using open spaces to substitute for punctuation. Strive for regularity from one stanza to another, but feel free to vary the 5-stanza, 5-line format.

Sample Poems

Grass

Who's kept receipts anyway
things you've learned over these years
growth you've sung into the grass
never doubting sun and rain to not agree
what steps to grow what patience set free

why throw dough to some stranger
when you can spread the seed or at least
start using the rototiller
sweating over the inches
spreading over the daunting dirt

so many weekends to foster new year's lawn
fertilizer for the poking patches
tall fescue perennial rye
manual hose automatic display
and tools I cannot even say

sun and water and more seed
depend on you
to know how to apply
and bring back to life
lean on you never to die

—Jennifer Kosuda

Father's Day Gardening

For you it is hauling up the hoses
coiled in the basement like garter snakes
that forgot to stop growing   through whose loops
like massive bangles you hook your arm
the dangling ends clattering up the steps behind you

and the galvanized bucket filled with hose toys
such as stretchy washers like forgiving rings
I can wiggle onto my fingers and brass
couplings with their swirly threads to link
male and female ends and then and then

you screw the male end into the frost-free bib
of the house sillcock with its ball valves
levers and handles and fittings and adapters
and when there are no more kinks in the hose
no more missing ends   no more punctures

no more leaking or fear of blowout force
you pull my end over to me and you turn on
the water so the surge leaps up the hose
makes it taut with pressure for me
to swivel the head to shower the petunias

to jet clean my bucket   to soak the dried out
dahlia bed and quench the thirst of cucumbers
moisten all that can bloom   sprout   unfurl   bolt
climb as I wave the wand spluttering   shooting
misting the garden into quivering life.

—Susanna Rich

Craft Tip #26: Top Down, Bottom Up

—Alan Michael Parker

I have come to believe that too many poems start too slowly and go too long—especially the contemporary lyric poems I tend to write. In these poems, the first few lines set the scene, similar to how an establishing shot operates in a movie, and then the action starts. In the last few lines, the movie gains an orchestra, and the poem ramps up its dramatic and emotional tension in the name of making the ending more profound. Of course, I'm not accusing the writers (read: me) of writing such poems as an act of chicanery, but of using a mode of rhetorical excess that deploys a framing device in misguided ways. It's a mix of didacticism, lyricism, and the quest for the epiphany that don't always mix well.

What to do? *Top down, bottom up.* My suggestion for revision, with an eye on those less-effective phenomena, is to cut as many lines from the beginning (*top down*) and the ending (*bottom up*) that can be cut. Cut what you can get away with cutting; find the beginning that launches us and the ending that offers satisfaction without bluster or sentimentality. Tighten the poem into an experience rather than stage an experience. *Top down, bottom up.*

Now let's consider one of the consequences of this maneuver—while admitting, of course, that it's not a panacea. While *top down, bottom up* often works, it does so differently each time. And that's because this idea's not exclusively a strategy to eliminate rhetorical excess or trim all rhetoric from the lyric's operation. I'm not suggesting that the poem has to be unframed, the page its only context. Nevertheless, especially when thinking of the forms of chat and speech that have entered poetry as musical ideas in contemporary free verse, *top down, bottom up* may, in fact, facilitate finding the music lurking in the existing syntax and focusing upon that music.

Top down, bottom up is not the same suggestion as *Kill your darlings.* I'm not saying that the first and last few lines always contain precious moments that derail the poem, moments you love and would be loath to eliminate. This is a different idea. So, even more unorthodoxically, once you cut these lines in the manner I'm suggesting, see if they can be used in smaller ways within the poem that's still there. That is, trim these phrases or parts of phrases from the beginning and the ending, and then re-introduce the smallest possible portions of them elsewhere. In other words, consider what among the phrases or word-pairs or images or ideas that have been cut are *necessary*, and might be grafted to the poem.

Ultimately, *top down, bottom up* may have led you to cut stunningly fabulous writing that would further the poem's successes, and the poem would prosper by having the crucial portions of this writing reintroduced elsewhere within the same text.

Poem and Prompt

Pulse

My flight is heading for Zurich
when the killer opens fire

in a Florida night club. I'll hold
my newborn grandson in my arms

as soon as I reach Florence,
                              but right now
someone is killing people

                in pre-dawn Orlando
while it's broad daylight here.

Dozens dead, hostages, pools of blood,
I still don't know, haven't yet arrived

where love is bringing me.
                In Orlando
a man who slapped his wives around
shouts a pledge into his phone

and guns down young people
                he doesn't even know.

How can the finite quantities
            of love in this world
                          be blown apart
on a party floor of dancing friends?

Little one,
            I'll hold you in my arms,
sing you lullabies and show tunes,

when a new love is born
it's worth crossing an ocean for.

Whoever you turn out to be,
sweet boy,
who can protect you?

—Maxine Susman

Susman presents us with two parallel actions: the personal story of the speaker's flight to Zurich to meet her new grandchild and the public story of the Pulse night club shooting in Orlando, Florida. Throughout the poem she juxtaposes the two stories, moving back and forth from one to the other and weaving them together.

The poet uses first person. She also uses present tense which is made more interesting as there's a time difference between Orlando and where the speaker is in her travels: it's *pre-dawn in Orlando / while it's broad daylight here*.

The contrast between time in one location and time in another underscores the larger contrasts between birth and death and between love and hate.

Notice also the use of questions. The first question appears in stanza 8; it conveys the speaker's bafflement as well as the irony that exists in this world, that love and hate can co-exist. The second question, this one at the end of the poem, is a direct address to the baby: *Whoever you turn out to be / sweet boy, / who can protect you?* The speaker leaves us without an answer.

The zigzag form of the poem is ideal for conveying the feeling of travel from one place to another. It also emphasizes the several contrasts as the speaker goes back and forth from one story to the other.

Let's try a poem of juxtaposition. First, freewrite for 5-10 minutes about a personal story, a current one or an older one that remains important to you.

Next, find a story in the news, one that grips you. Freewrite about it for 5-10 minutes.

Your challenge is to discover a connection between the two stories, between the personal and the public. As you write your draft, weave the two stories together, going back and forth from one to the other.

Use first person and present tense.

Include some opposites, some contrasts.

Ask 1-2 questions.

Use a direct address.

Find a format for your poem that enhances its content.

Sample Poems

What We Women Put Ourselves Through

I paid $1000 to have my face lasered—burned, really—
turning me into a lizard, then the whole shebang
peeled for a week. Not the onion paper
peel of a sunburn but dehydrated onion flakes
like dandruff from forehead to chin, ear to ear.

On Mother's Day, a Facebook link reported
A human body can bear up to 45 del of pain.
Yet when giving birth, a mother feels 57 del of pain—
similar to 20 bones breaking at once.
Turns out, it was fake news: There's no such unit as a del.
Childbirth is more like Jeff Foxworthy's description:
a wet St. Bernard coming in through the cat door,
or if you're one of 6 percent, you have an
orgasm during birth.

My camp roommate was afraid of sex
because her aunt had told her it was the most
excruciating pain she'd ever felt.
When I was in grade school and my sister explained
the man has to get on top of the lady, I dismissed it: No way
our obese principal could lie
on his petite wife without squashing her.

Luckily, I, like 50 percent of women, have forgotten the pain
of labor. Joyous relief, or the *halo effect*
replaces it, ensuring we won't fear doing it again—
necessary, given the stats in the old days.
Half of children died before their fifth birthday
in 1800, and in 15th-century Florence,
women made out their wills
as soon as pregnancy was confirmed.

Now I'm undergoing a *total body skin pampering experience:*
pure coconut oil and papaya green tea
with a soothing wrap of warmed paraffin.
The attendant tells me to strip and warns it will
be hot, but then it really IS hot, scalding, as in torturous,
as in get this off me, NOW.
She leaves me mummified, my claustrophobic self
lying here sweating in a small dark tomb.

But I'm thinking of how Mona Lisa has no brows or lashes
because women plucked them out. Vital back then
and now not to be *unsightly.*
God forbid we have an extra hair anywhere
beside our heads. I'll stay put for my next waxing ordeal.
They say it helps to cough as each strip rips the offenders
from their roots. 85 dels of pain.
A chicken being plucked for the pot.

—Karen Paul Holmes

Women Whose Fathers Died in December

I hate the ringtone that wakes us at 4 a.m. Dad has died.
    The mammogram alarmed my doctor.
It will take days to ship the body from Germany to Newark.
    They called me in for extra views.
Upstairs, while the kids trim the tree, I call my friend Mariel.
    I read every article, interviewed other doctors.
Did you choose to look at your father's body? I don't want to.
    I kept my phone with me every second.
Am I wrong? Will I regret it? What's the right way to mourn?
    Workers repaired our street's sidewalks.
We've bought presents for him, he's wrapped his for us.
    I realized I might not outlast them.
I use the tissues too quickly, need a towel to bury cries.
    I wondered if I'd see my kids graduate.
The hours are full of phone calls and visits and errands.
    I hadn't wanted to worry my parents.
Taking care of Mom occupies me. What'll I do after she dies?
    It took too long to hear any news.
Any radio could start playing "Have Yourself a Merry Little..."
    I heard I was fine the day after Dad died.

—Tina Kelley

Craft Tip #27: The Shallow and the Deep: How to Revise a Group of Poems

—Nicole Cooley

Revising individual poems can be quite different from reworking and rethinking a collection: a chapbook, a sequence, or a full-length collection of poems. This kind of revision poses new and delightful challenges.

In so many ways, revising poems as a group is my favorite kind of revision. I love to think about juxtaposition, disjunction, collision, and connection—that is, I believe so much in the deep pleasure of working on poems in groups. As a writer and as a teacher, I like this kind of revision most because it is—maybe paradoxically—the most liberating.

Whenever I think of revision, I always return to Adrienne Rich's definition of revision as a true re-vision: *entering an old text from a new critical direction*. This is the pain and pleasure of revision, this revisitation. The question is how to see your work with fresh eyes. This can be so difficult, especially when you are looking at a group of poems.

But I love the idea of re-entering a text. As if, as poet Minnie Bruce Pratt has asserted, a poem is a room. If I am revising, I can't necessarily re-enter through the front door. I may need to break in, to sneak under a door, to break down dry wall, to blow out the roof.

And perhaps a collection is, in fact, a very large room, with more space, and more walls to potentially take down, more windows to remove.

With Rich and Pratt in mind, there are two crucial—and fun—methods I employ when revising my own group of poems for a collection. I think of these methods as the shallow and the deep, and I know that both are necessary to the kind of revision I want to do, the kind of revision that is so much more than editing, the kind of revision that is about cracking open the poems and truly re-seeing them anew.

1. First, I consider the shallow (not a pejorative term!). For me the delight in revising a group of poems is thinking across poems, without diving deeply into a single poem but rather interviewing my poems and asking the group of poems a series of questions:

- What color is this group of poems?
- If this group of poems had a favorite food, what would it be?
- What music do these poems love best?
- If these poems could speak to me about their greatest problems, what would they say?
- What could these poems tell me about how to rework my life, to work harder on them?
- What should I do differently?

2. Then there is the deep. So often deep thinking about poems takes me back to definitions and origins. Which takes me to the dictionary, the OED most of all.

One way to go deep is to review your group of poems and write down three to four key themes that reverberate in your work. For example, in my case, writing my last collection, I wrote: Escape, Save, Money, Sequester. Then without looking back at the poems in the collection, I went right to the dictionary. I wrote out each definition of each word. Then I worked with that language, the linguae of the word's origin, to write a poem. I used the title "Of_____" as a placeholder ("Of Escape," etc.)

As I do this kind of dictionary work, what I have found is that this dictionary excavation leads to many discoveries. As I am doing when I most often write my best work, I am not trying to *write a poem* (or a poem with a capital *P*). With no agenda in mind—though I am revising!—I am free to re-invent, reformulate, and reconceive. These poems may end up in the manuscript or they may most often just lead to deeper thinking about the themes and language of my work.

Both the shallow and the deep have led me to a different way of thinking of and through revision. A way of revising that is productive and engaging.

We are not fixing or editing our poems when we revise, especially when we revise a group of poems. Instead, we are taking risks of language and form and meaning. We are going places in our work we did not know we would go. We are challenging ourselves to write the best poems that we may not feel capable of writing, the poems we are meant to write.

Poem and Prompt

Epicurean

A hungry mouth, an empty mouth, insistent mouth,
mouth that would be filled by the seaweed of me,
that would crack the shell with a rock and take
its portion. The mouth gages its slide, gapes—
grotto mouth. Mouth where I might go to pray,
to fall upon my knees before. A mouth full of yes,
singer of heights and sorrows, Swannanoa of
a mouth. French Broad, Pigeon, a mouth so wet,
sweet as a North Carolina river. A mouth that keeps
its secrets like a mountain still. Moonshine mouth,
mouth of fiddles and laments. Yes, a mouth that knows
itself. Generous. No virgin's pout, nor a greedy boy's
insistence. Give me one that has been already schooled.
Not excess, but experience.
      Epicurus did not advocate for wine,
      but for salt of the skin,
and water to quench it. Paradox but not duplicity.
In my awe I would have this honest mouth, dive into the bliss
of it. Speechless mouth that makes its desires plain—
      Who wouldn't want to
draw from this cup the well? Give me a mouth
I might place my own chapped lips to in the heat
of summer. A mouth to sate, to surrender.

—Vievee Francis

Francis has written a poem of extravagant praise. Notice the
repetition of the word *mouth*. How effectively the repetition
conveys the speaker's obsession with that body part. Notice the
hyperbolic metaphors, e.g., *Mouth where I might go to pray*
and the comparison of the mouth to a mansion, then to rivers,
then to a mountain.

It's interesting to note how the poet, at the midway point, swings into telling us what the mouth is *not*: *No virgin's pout, nor a greedy boy's insistence.*

Note also the allusion to Epicurus to add authority to the speaker's hunger for the mouth—and the indentation to draw attention to that.

Notice, too, how the poet alternates complete sentences with fragments. The heaping on of fragments suggests an outpouring of feeling, of powerful desire.

Finally, notice how one part of the body represents the entire figure of the beloved. What a perfect use of synecdoche.

✐ ✐ ✐

For your own poem, choose a body part and let it represent the person you are lusting after or would like to be lusting after. Neck, ear, arm, ankle? Make a list of things—places, objects, aspects of Nature—you might compare the body part to. Let that list evolve into a list of metaphors.

Using Google, do a bit of research on your body part. Jot down notes on material that might enter your poem. Be on the lookout especially for something that might serve as an allusion. Another way to find an allusion might be to google something like *quotations about the ear.*

Now compose your first draft, using the material you've gathered. Let it roll out. Gush a bit. Be passionate, extravagant, hyperbolic. Work in some negatives. Try your hand at some strategic repetition and use of fragments.

Feel free, if you prefer, to save the research part for after the first draft is written. Do the gushing first.

Sample Poems

Treasure

after Vievee Francis's "Epicurean"

A broad chest, a barrel chest, chest that Atlas
wished to have before he hefted the world's weight
onto his shoulders. A chest that I would fill
with the pearls and gold doubloons of my love,
that I would fight Ali Baba and the 40 thieves
to take as my own. A chest whose sublime musculature
Michelangelo, even with the finest Carrara marble,
would be hard-pressed to chisel and replicate.

Not the mothball-laden metal chest of my childhood
where wool blankets and winter socks were kept,
but a chest of blood and bone and flesh
that, from neck to navel, my lips would kiss clean each night.
In my adoration, I would have this chest, enter with reverence
its cave of wonders, both losing and finding myself
there in the riches of my beloved's secrets, the breath of his life,
and, the greatest treasure, his heart.

—Shayla Hawkins

Eye to Eye

Give me that sidelong look, give me
that crinkled eye, curved as an almond, dark
as vanilla. Oh, surrender your glance, your gaze,
your chestnut eye, sweet as kiwi, round as coconut.
Eye like agate, like geode a girl
breaks open, clapping for what hides
inside. Eye of newt dropped into a bubbling potion,
inflicting mischief or love or love's revenge.
Eye of giant squid whose courting habits
are discourteous, eye of Brookesia micra who inhabits
an uninhabited island, her mating rituals
never seen by a naked
human eye. I call you
apple of my eye and so can call you
Honeycrisp, Ambrosia, my Delicious.
Give me your majestic eye, your exceptional eye,
your superlunary eye.
Give me your sumptuous eye, your transcendent eye.
Emerson advised he would become
a transparent eyeball, but I prefer
your opaque amber iris, your perfect pupil.
So long as we can breathe, or eyes can see,
drink to me only. Raise a toast
with demitasse cups, crystal tumblers, cut-glass goblets.
Lift your magnums, your Jeroboams, your Nebuchadnezzars.
Be my witness. Eye that watches me tumble
clumsily as Jack or Jill, fall greatly off a wall,
eye that puts me back together again.

—Lynn Domina

Top Tips: Bilgere's Best

—George Bilgere

1. Write about what you don't know. Yes! Be willing to upend the old *write what you know* bromide and tackle something you wouldn't ordinarily consider to be subject matter for a poem. Read a book of poems by Alice Fulton or Thomas Lux and you'll see how they find poetry in the oddest and most far-fetched corners of the world. I mean, how many more poems about your divorce or your father's drinking does the world really need? (pointing a finger here at you, Bilgere!).

2. Buy yourself one of those tiny binder notebooks, small enough to fit in a back pocket or a purse, and as you go through the day jot down any odd random thought or observation that might have the germ of a poem in it. Then (see number three):

3. Get up in the morning, sit down at your writing desk, pull out your little notebook—and voilà! You don't have to waste time thinking up something to write about. You have three or four ideas staring you right in the face. Or (see number four):

4. Or don't sit down at your writing table. Instead, amble down to a cozy little local café with your writing notebook. Order a cup of coffee and a croissant. And write your morning poem right there at the café. A change of venue can really help. Which brings me to number five:

5. Write your morning poem! If you're lucky enough to be facing a period of free time (we teachers get three whole months!), take advantage of it by writing every single day. Morning is my best time, and it's probably yours.

6. If you're in the habit of writing on a laptop, try changing this up by getting yourself one of those sumptuous big 8"x11" artist sketch books. Unlined. Get a nice gel pen (I love gel pens, fine point in particular). Poems were not meant to be composed on a computer! Leave your laptop at home and head for the café armed only with your gel pen and notebook.

7. Get yourself in the mood for writing by reading the work of a poet who really excites you about poetry. I'll look at something by Marie Howe, Louis Jenkins, Tony Hoagland, Dorianne Laux, something that makes me think, *This is fantastic! I want to do this too!*

8. This one's pretty obvious, but for me it's essential: make sure you have an audience for your work. Your husband, wife, lover, best friend, writing group, whatever. I need to know that my efforts might be rewarded by a *Wow!* or *That's a beauty* by my wife that evening. And yes, I realize there's a good chance she'll look up from the poem with that expression I know so well and say, *Sorry. Not this time.* Which is okay, since whether she likes the poem or not it's five o'clock and time for a glass of wine!

9. Make sure that at any given moment you have at least ten groups of poems circulating among the journals that might like and publish your work. And it goes without saying that you need to educate yourself about what those journals are. If you're not doing this, why are you writing?

10. I love to head down to my favorite little independent bookstore here in Cleveland of a summer afternoon and browse through the poetry section. I muse over various old and new collections of poetry, I look for new writers, and I never leave without buying a book of poetry. I think all of us writers owe it to the poetry world, the literature world, the wonderful world of bookstores, to buy a book every week. When you actually slap down your money or your credit card for a book of poetry, the whole enterprise seems suddenly more serious, more genuine, more essential. After all, you buy food, don't you? Why not poetry? And if you really like the book, take the trouble to find the poet's email and send a fan letter! Nothing makes a poet happier than knowing that she or he is actually being read and appreciated somewhere out there in the world.

Bonus Prompt: The Revision Infusion Poem

Go to the folder where you keep your drafts of poems that failed but still hold some value for you. Pull out one you want to work with.

Now grab a journal or a collection of poems by someone else. Sit down and read until you come to a poem you really like, one with wonderful, distinctive language. Circle five fabulous words in that poem.

Now return to your draft and find places to insert those words into your poem. Scatter the words throughout your draft. This activity should open up all kinds of new possibilities. It might very well lead you to a radical revision of your draft. It might also lead you to a poem you now love.

X. Publishing Your Book

After the final no there comes a yes.
And on that yes the future world depends.

—Wallace Stevens

Craft Tip #28: How to Order Your Poetry Manuscript

—April Ossmann

In my experience, the biggest mystery to emerging and sometimes established poets is how to effectively order a poetry manuscript. It requires a different kind of thinking: a helicopter or three-dimensional view, as opposed to the two-dimensional thinking necessary for line editing poems. Ordering requires seeing each poem from a distance, so all its sides are visible, and seeing the manuscript as a whole, how each poem might connect with others in a series.

The first consideration is the inclusion and exclusion of poems, a critical part of ordering, and perhaps the most difficult, because it can mean letting go of emotional attachments. Sometimes, we keep a poem because it represents an important emotional phase or event or because it's the title poem, ignoring the inner voice whispering it's not up to snuff. Sometimes, it feels important to the collection's narrative or themes or it was published in a magazine. There are only two inseparable criteria that should govern: The poem is strong *and* fits the major or minor themes and subjects, helping to create a cohesive whole. If a poem doesn't fit the criteria, save it for a future manuscript, for rereading, or framing as a broadside—but don't leave it in the manuscript. Strength, not length, makes a good book.

When contemplating poem inclusion, consider strong uncollected new poems, which may not feel as if they belong. When I edit a manuscript, I give each poem a grade: check-plus, check, or check-minus. Then I set aside the check-minuses. If there are enough check-pluses to create a book-length manuscript, I set aside the checks, too—after deciding whether they can be edited up to check-pluses, giving special consideration to those with thematic importance and to rough drafts with strong potential.

I reread the poems, listing each one's themes and subjects and noting repeated words or images. Such repetitions can be a strength or a weakness—or both. Next, I separate the poems based on theme or subject, and count how many of the strongest landed in each pile, using that as one of multiple guides to a successful ordering. I'm not a believer in one perfect way to order a manuscript. Try inventing strategies beyond those I suggest, choosing one particular to the poetic style, themes, subjects, obsessions, strengths, and weaknesses of the poems. Try different strategies and make a decision based on both intellect and intuition, but go with the ordering that *feels* right.

In working with Adrian Matejka to edit *The Devil's Garden* (Alice James Books), the original manuscript had a roughly narrative/ chronological ordering, including many subjects and themes, but a strong common thread: identity. The final ordering highlights that thread, delineating how music/musicians, history, art, pop culture, ethnic background, family, and experience formed the speaker's identity. Subjects are interwoven throughout, ordered to create a sense of growth or evolution (not chronology—the poems flash forward and back in time, reflecting how the mind experiences identity), resulting in a thematically cohesive collection.

Ordering strategies I've used include creating a narrative line or arc (regardless of whether the poetry is narrative) and grouping or interweaving themes to create a sense of evolution or growth toward a conclusion—not resolution. Another strategy is a lyric ordering in which each poem links to the previous, sharing a word, image, subject, or theme. This sometimes provides a continuation, sometimes a contrast or argument. Sometimes, I follow an emotionally charged poem with one providing comic or other relief; and sometimes I interweave the poetic styles, individual poem length, pace, tone, or emotion. Some orderings build toward a narrative, emotional, or evolutionary climax or conclusion; and some end deliberately unresolved or ambiguous. Different poetic styles can benefit from different ordering considerations. A manuscript composed of deliberately non-narrative poems, might best be ordered according to a strategy of collage, surprise, or juxtaposition—or by creating a faux narrative arc.

Other considerations include whether to heighten or downplay repetition of imagery, words, or subjects. If there are too many repetitions of a word or image, I recommend making some substitutions and placing those poems at strategic intervals in the manuscript. This can create a subtle sense of obsession rather than a numbing one. I alternate strong and less strong poems, and avoid having too many poems in a row on the same subject or theme, except where they indicate growth, contrast, or argument. I may order to heighten the importance and relevance of the manuscript's title or leitmotif or to create a greater sense of thematic unity. Generally my suggested order juggles most of these concerns at once, which is where that three-dimensional or helicopter view is most critical.

To achieve an order that maximizes strengths and minimizes weaknesses, it's crucial to gain the editorial distance necessary to self-evaluate, to think like an editor. An exercise for achieving this is listing a minimum of two strengths and weaknesses per poem, i.e.: syntax, diction, voice; too much or not enough description; the balance of abstract to concrete imagery or symbolism; the flow or rhythm; the presence or lack of tension or risk (narrative, dramatic, linguistic, formal, emotional); the capacity to surprise; line breaks; word choice (the most accurate, evocative choice); point of view; and the use or misuse of dialogue. Noting as many strengths and weaknesses as possible allows for the most objective evaluation of which poems are strongest and why.

I consider whether a manuscript needs sections and whether they will benefit from titles. The current convention tends toward untitled sections, which works for many, but not all manuscripts. Some progressions are best not interrupted, and some collections don't require the extra breathing space. Valerie Martínez's *Each and Her* (University of Arizona Press) is a perfect example of both. The poems, ordered as a numbered series without sections, are exceptionally spare and employ metaphor, collage, lists, found poems, fragments, and juxtaposition, all revolving around an emotionally charged subject—the murdered women of Juárez—to create a fractured, incomplete narrative and a tense, riveting progression.

For sectioned manuscripts, I begin and end each one with strong poems that create links between sections. It's important to begin and end the manuscript with two of the strongest poems, but I also recommend giving consideration to which subjects, themes, or poetic styles best introduce the poet's work and the speaker's character, and what the poet considers to be the crucial *takeaway* for the reader. Which lines does the poet want to ring in the reader's ears on closing the book—which are most worthy and memorable?

I don't often recommend titling sections, because it often feels too telling, directive, or limiting of potential interpretations, especially for accessible poetic styles. Titling sections for such manuscripts works best when it heightens ambiguities or adds to potential interpretations rather than explains. Titling sections for more elliptical poetry styles can be a boon for the reader, offering an assist without spoiling the mystery.

Other ordering conventions include prologue or epilogue poems, epigraphs, and notes, all of which can add to or detract from a manuscript's strengths. My expectation for a prologue is that it be one of the strongest and most representative poems in the collection, yet poets often choose a weak one, placing it in the most visible position. Title poems create a similarly oft-disappointed expectation. In such cases, I recommend that the poet omit or line edit and retitle the poem, but keep the original title as the book title. Epilogue poems rarely seem necessary to me, but can be a fine or fun choice where their use is humorous or they offer a bit of the after-story, but it still risks feeling overly intentional or clever—or unnecessary.

Epigraphs have been such an enduring convention that many poets seem to feel they're required for a book to be taken seriously. As both rebel and reformer, I take issue with real or imagined strictures, but some authors and readers simply love epigraphs. For me, they work best where they highlight, comment on, or expand on a theme, subject, or obsession in the manuscript, but if the poet has done good work, an epigraph shouldn't be *necessary*.

Once I've ordered a manuscript, I let it steep overnight and read it again the next day to see if the ordering still seems good. I recommend that authors do this on a more elastic timeline: Try reading the manuscript at odd moments over a period of days or weeks. Try printing several versions employing different orderings, and then use intuition to decide which one is best.

Poem and Prompt

Portrait with Closed Eyes

She was the stain in the teacup
  that spread up toward the handle.
She was the handle that snapped
  off the hairbrush, and
She was the hairbrush he tossed
  onto the fire, and
She was the fire he carried
  each day in his pipe.

She was the pipe the bath water
  rode to the river, and
She was the river where they
  boarded the boat to limbo.
She was the limbo that held
  the secrets of acorns, and
She was the acorn that
  bruised his weary knees.

She was the knees that knocked
  beneath the oak table, and
She was the table where glasses
  were refilled till midnight.
She was the midnight that darkened
  the brow of the child,
Child who never felt safe indoors,
  who never felt safe outdoors.

She, the heaviest of doors, was the reason.
  She was their stain.

           —Jeanne Marie Beaumont

In her portrait poem, Beaumont describes her subject in a series of metaphors. She immediately sets up a pattern of sentences beginning with *She was* and concluding with a metaphor. The anaphora of *She was* creates not only pattern but also rhythm.

Notice that the pattern is broken towards the end of stanza 3 as line 7 of that stanza begins with *Child who*. The closing stanza, only two lines, is also a departure from the poem's pattern. The first three stanzas contain eight lines each, but this last one, while it contains the *She was* beginning, interrupts the pattern with a modifying phrase, thus making us wait for the metaphor.

Notice that the last line of the poem repeats the word *stain*, circling us back to line 1.

Another kind of repetition is the use of compound sentences joined by *and*. This syntactical device also contributes to the pattern and to the music of the poem.

Beaumont formats the poem into an artistic arrangement on the page. But it's more than just pretty; it's also sensible. The first half of the sentence begins flush to the left margin. The sentence then breaks at the end of the line and the remainder gets indented on the next line. The first line of each sentence is not end-stopped which pushes us forward to the continuation in the next line. One line flows into the next.

Perhaps the most interesting use of repetition is *anadiplosis*— the repetition of a prominent word, usually the last word in one phrase or clause, at the beginning of the next phrase or clause. For example, line 2 ends with *handle*. That word is reiterated in the next line's metaphor. Beaumont takes liberties with this technique as she pulls her word from anywhere in the first part of the sentence and repeats it anywhere in the second half of the sentence. The result of this technique is a poem structurally full of unity and musically full of echoes.

✎ ✎ ✎

For your own portrait poem, first find a photo or painting of a man or a woman, or just choose someone you know or have seen. Any age is fine.

Begin your first line with a phrase that you will repeat throughout the poem. It might be *She was* or *He was*, or feel free to switch to present tense—*He is* or *She is*. You will find it easier to compose the metaphors if you use a state-of-being verb. Similes are also fine, e.g., *She looked like* or *He seemed like*.

Try your hand at anadiplosis. Select a word from your first metaphor and use it to initiate the next metaphor. Work with this technique throughout your draft. This can't help but stimulate your imagination.

As you move to subsequent drafts, hone your metaphors, keeping the best ones and improving them, kicking the weak ones to the curb.

You might want to imitate Beaumont's artistic arrangement of lines on the page, especially if you've never used such a pattern. Or find your own arrangement.

Be sure to vary your pattern somewhere in the poem. Why? Because poems often profit from it. You keep your readers on their toes. Just when they've come to expect one thing, you toss out a different thing. Surprise your readers.

Sample Poems

Portrait of Her in the Window

She was the crack in the serving tray
   that delivered sugared almonds.
She was the almonds that littered
   the dessert table, and
She was the table they hauled
   to the dump in the rain, and
She was the rain that blinded
   them when they drove to the sea.

She was the sea denuding
   the shore after storms, and
She was the storm she called forth
   every time she closed her eyes.
She was the closed eye that guarded
   the kingdom of secrets and
She was the secret that
   put stones in their mouths.

She was the mouth that opened
   like a bird in hunger, and
She was the hunger that prowled
   the house like a shadow.
She was the shadow that drifted
   through her own dreams,
Dreams that came like storms
   to beat against the window.

She was the window. She was
   the crack in the pane. She was
the condensation each time it rained.

—Jennifer Saunders

284

Swept

My hands grip handle, pendulum
swing on Grandmama's steps, broom
falls apart at the seams. I the broom,
the unsewn seam. Her dime gripped,
this good job of work swept through

time, spending the peace between
women and men. I the steps Granddaddy
trips, belly beerful, his way undone.
I the storm's eye, this good work,
this right on time, for Buffalo nickel

or dime. Sweep it gone, this dust
of a girl who spins on the head of a pin.
I the rust, the splinter, swept under carpet
or rug, bone in my arm unable to rest.
I the dirt hidden and piled, song

for my supper, this house of uneasy
belong. Now I the woman disturbing
the peace, my handle gripped, I the web
husband leaves in the eaves, spidering
book and shelf. I the broomstraw

stuck in his craw, cain raised in cloud
of days. I the pendulum sweeping him
gone, coin of the realm outspending
our fine design. I the hands, the railing
tripped, I the seam unknowing the rip.

I the steps leapt two at a time, we
the bellyful having enough. I the eye
gathering storms, the peace swept here
alone. I the haze, tune unhummed,
that good clean sweep the long way home.

—Linda Parsons
published in *The Meadow*

Craft Tip #29: The Work of Promoting Your Poetry Book

—Diane Lockward

Once your manuscript is within months of publication, it's time to think about promotion. If your collection is with a large publishing house, you may receive the services of a marketing department with a budget, but if you, like most of us, have your book with a small press, your publisher will have little or no budget for promotion. If you want your book to find its way into the hands of readers, you will need to work to make that happen. Ideally, promotion will be a collaborative effort between you and your publisher, but don't count on that. In many instances, promotion will be your job.

Getting Ready to Promote Your Book

While you wait for your book to get published, prepare to do an email blitz. Compile an up-to-date email list. Your list should include hundreds, not dozens, of recipients. Don't exclude anyone thinking this or that person won't be interested. Sometimes the least likely person will purchase your book, while your old pal won't bother. Include all your friends, everyone you've ever met in the poetry community, people who've been in workshops with you, everyone in your grad school program, all your former teachers, anyone who's ever sent you a nice note about your poetry, even your neighbors.

If you don't already have a website, get one. A page at your publisher's site is not enough. You need your own website. You can get a domain name very inexpensively. Since this is your website's address, use your own name so people can easily locate your website. You can get a hosting site inexpensively or for free. Popular ones are Word Press, Go Daddy, Wix, and Weebly. If possible, design your own site so that you can maintain and update it yourself. If you use a web designer, you will, of course, pay for the service, but don't go wild.

Your website should include a bio, sample poems, links to other poems, and contact information. Be sure your website is attractive, free of ads, and always up-to-date. Use your website to generate advance buzz. Announce there that your book is forthcoming. Add a cover image once you have one. Provide a release date once you have one. Have pages ready for links to online reviews and interviews and a calendar of your readings.

Spreading the Word

The email blitz is the single most important thing you can do to get your book off to a good start. Once your book is listed on such sites as Amazon and Barnes & Noble, send an email announcement with your cover image, a brief blurb, and a purchase link that goes directly to your book's listing page (make it easy for people to buy your book). This information should be in the body of your email message. Do not add an attachment as many people will not open it. Send out the announcement in batches over a period of days.

Later, when you get a feature somewhere or a review or interview, repeat your blitz. Share the good news. It doesn't matter if people receive more than one notice about your book. Readers often need to see the title of a book multiple times before deciding to buy. Many recipients will appreciate—and act upon—the reminder.

If your publisher does not design a press release for you, design one yourself. Include a cover image, brief bio, one blurb, purchase information, and contact information. This should be no more than one page. Go through your Acknowledgments page and check the website of each journal that first published the poems that now appear in your new book. See what each journal's review policy is. If the journal accepts review copies for consideration, send one. With each review copy, include a press release and a note asking for review consideration. Remind the editor that a particular poem first appeared in his journal. Address the editor by name. Hopefully, your publisher will provide you with review copies to mail out, but if not, buy some copies at your discounted rate; this is a good investment.

Also send the press release to your college alumni newsletter. Put one up on the bulletin board where you work. Fire off some to local libraries and bookstores. Send another with a fact sheet to your local newspaper; request an article and offer to go in for an interview. Send a press release to the local paper of any town where you used to live.

Lining Up Readings

Readings are essential if you hope to sell books. Let your first reading be a book launch party. Invite your relatives, friends, neighbors, and poet pals. Have food. This reading may well be your best sales event as most people will come expecting to buy your book. If you have a friend with a book coming out around the same time, consider joining forces. Your local library may be willing to host your launch reading. Another wonderful way to launch your book is a literary salon held in someone's home.

To get additional readings, you need to compose a query letter. Keep it informative and succinct. Include links to your website and online sites where your work is available. Make a list of venues in your area. Send your query in the body of an email to bookstores, libraries, art galleries—all the usual places. Contact local book clubs and offer to present a reading and discussion for the group. If you have friends who teach, offer to do a reading, a Q&A, and a workshop. Apply to conferences, festivals, and book fairs. Then get creative. How about chocolate stores, museums, wine bars, and hip coffee shops?

Target groups that don't ordinarily attend readings but are somehow connected to your subject matter. Are your poems about flowers? Query nearby garden clubs and suggest a reading at one of their upcoming meetings. Do your poems deal with woman-related topics? Contact area women's clubs and the local branch of the AAUW. Are your poems about a particular ethnic group, for example, Italian-Americans? Contact your area Unico.

Eventually you will need to seek readings outside of your own area. Remember that the farther you cast your net, the fewer responses you're likely to get. Cast it anyhow, because you will get some responses. To locate venues, map out the distance you're willing to travel. Then do a Google search, for example, *poetry venues in New Jersey* or *poetry readings in Boston*. That should bring up some listings. If there's contact information, send off your query letter. Check out reading schedules on other poets' websites. Use these to suggest possible venues. Visit online calendars, such as those posted by the Academy of American Poets and Poets & Writers.

When you get readings, publicize them as widely as possible. List them in online calendars and send out email notices to people you know in the area of the reading. Do not rely solely on the venue host to drum up an audience for you.

Regardless of where you're reading, remember that you're promoting your book, so be prepared to read poems from the book. You may get tired of reading the same poems, but your audience will be hearing them for the first time. Your listeners will be more inclined to buy your book if you hold it and read from it. Remember, though, that not everyone who attends your reading will buy your book, so bring along oversized postcards with your cover image on one side and a poem and ordering information on the other. Give these out for free as some of the recipients might make a later purchase. These postcards can be ordered inexpensively from such online stores as Vistaprint.

Using the Internet

Join social networks such as Facebook, Twitter, Instagram, Pinterest, and Goodreads. These are hot gathering places for poets, and all are free. Accumulate friends and followers. Join sub-groups for poets. Announce your new book's publication in all your networks and groups. Through your social media contacts you will learn about reading venues as well as review and interview opportunities. You can also create event listings for your readings and send out invitations to your social contacts who live in the area of an upcoming reading. Be sure to use social media to share any good news about your book.

Another suggestion for your internet use, this one fast and easy: use your email signature to good advantage. Set your email program to automatically add a link to a purchase site for your book. Also include a link to your website at the bottom of each new message you write. If you like, you can add a link to your blog or anything special you have online such as a poem feature. Think of the signature area as free billboard space. You'll be amazed how many people will click on those links and go visiting.

Keeping Expectations Realistic

Promoting your book is the business of poetry, but don't expect to get rich. Remember that you're not looking for money—you're looking for an audience. It took you a long time, probably years, to write those poems and find a publisher. Your book deserves readers. It's easy to get discouraged when sales slow down as they inevitably will; remind yourself that poets sell their books one at a time, not by the dozens. If you plug away, your book will circulate. But to find readers, you need to be industrious, adventurous, persistent, and patient.

Poem and Prompt

Primrose Path

Can those be primroses traveling the cement
that winter cracked from one side of the driveway
to the other?—Two, three, four lilac-tinted blooms
sprouting from the jagged stretch of shallow dirt
as yet spared by random traffic and blind shoes,
not just surviving, in fact, but lavish in well-being,

awash with sun and dots of rainbow dew, twisting
this way and that in static dance, faces twisting

up as if to say, You see, you misguided being,
who needs kingdoms galore, who needs shoes
or love?—see us teeter here no hands along the dirt-
filled crack like kids on the loose, tilting in the bloom
of an April morning, death a lifetime of hours away
for any rogue primrose traveling the cement.

—Mark Smith-Soto

Smith-Soto employs an attractive and challenging variation of
the sonnet form. He gives us the traditional fourteen lines, but
the couplet appears in the middle of the poem, sandwiched
between two six-line stanzas. Instead of end rhymes, we have
end repetitions. It's this repetition business that is most interesting.
Notice that each end word in stanza 1 is repeated in stanza 3
but in reverse order.

Then notice that the two lines of stanza 2 both end with the
same word.

Notice, too, that both stanza 1 and stanza 3 begin with a question
and that the question mark is followed by a dash. Finally, notice

that after the first question the rest of the poem consists of one sentence. That sentence begins and then develops a description of the speaker's subject, the primroses growing up through a cement driveway.

For your own sidewalk sonnet, recall something amazing or unexpected that you saw on a sidewalk—or a path, a driveway, a trail, a road, a bridge. Begin your draft with a question from the first-person speaker about what he or she sees. Follow the question with a description of what is seen.

Now arrange what you've written into six lines followed by two lines. Each line of the two-line stanza should end with the same word.

When you feel reasonably satisfied with what you have written, put the end words of lines 1-6 into the end spots of six new lines (lines 9-14) but in reverse order. Now write those lines, beginning again with a question. Having the end words already in place may frustrate you but may also unlock fresh ideas.

In revision you might feel that some lines are weak or aren't working for some other reason. Change those lines, even if it means changing the end words. Remember that changing an end word in lines 1-6 will require a change in the corresponding line in the last stanza. Changing an end word in lines 9-14 will require a change in the corresponding line in the first stanza.

Think of this form as both limitation and opportunity.

Sample Poems

Territorial Rout

I think of my last meal. Thin as dust,
on the edge of my home, this frail mesa,
I am weary, wary of the roads
bull-dozed through my land, wide houses
surging where mesquite and juniper
once provided cover. The jackrabbits
dwindle, move west, but how far, how far?
My eyes have yellowed, developed a far-
away glaze, barely noticing jackrabbits
arcing down arroyos. Age-old juniper
chainsawed to make room for a house,
or a view for a house, or another road—
humans, those who now claim this mesa.
My heart, my bones, my land scraped to dust.

—Scott Wiggerman

Wormageddon

Can those be earthworms scattered about here and there
on a thin film of water risen from the saturated soil?—
Five, ten, hundreds of layabouts on the driveway,
shades of purple, rose, and bloodless gray intestines
sprinkled haphazardly, but curved into themselves, like spoons,
only too sickly-looking and waterlogged, even for birds

to eat the worn partygoers, achy and hungover, sleeping,
strewn like some kind of confetti, drugged, sleeping

the sleep of the dead, not even the peeping of birds,
returned north to mate could wake, not even a giant spoon could
spare them the drenched earth, the bloated intestines,
how could I not think Pollock abandoned the worms on my driveway,
airbrushed worms that surfaced like boats in locks, from saturated soil,
only to meet the fate of tires here, of feet there.

—Carla Schwartz

Craft Tip #30: Protocol for Poetry Readings

—Adele Kenny

As director of the long-running Carriage House Poetry Series, I've heard many, many poets read. Some have given great readings, and some haven't. I know that every poet wants to do well, and I've observed that some of the best share common elements of reading presentation.

The way a poem sounds is important, and poetry readings bring poets into closer contact with their audiences than the printed word allows. With the exception of spoken word poets, poets are not typically performers, but reading with spirit and communicating your enjoyment of poetry is important for a successful reading.

Following are some tips on how to enhance the success of your readings:

1. Prepare well. Select the poems you plan to read and rehearse them several times. Read the poems to yourself, follow the guidelines given by punctuation for pausing and stressing, and honor your line breaks. Listen to each poem's musicality and try to match your voice to it. If you have a video camera or voice recorder, you can tape yourself during practice. You can also stand in front of a mirror (full-length is good) and observe yourself as you read.

2. In preparing your set, variety is key. Start and end with your best poems, and keep in mind that some levity is always good to change the pace after reading somber poems. Follow long poems with shorter ones. Time yourself while rehearsing to make sure your reading will fit the time allotted to you. Overkill is deadly. Always leave the audience wanting more.

3. If seeing clearly is an issue, print your poems out in a large font and read from that hard copy. Mark pauses and breath or stress points with a highlighter to help you remember what you rehearsed. On the subject of rehearsing, be sure to have all your

materials ready. Watching a poet thumb through pages looking for a poem to read can be annoying and will appear amateurish.

4. Before the reading begins, if the host doesn't offer you a spot to place your books for sale, it's fair to ask for one. If the host doesn't tell the audience that your books are for sale, it's perfectly fine to tactfully tell the audience yourself. Be sure to offer to sign books. Being gracious goes a long way and makes you look less like you're pushing for sales.

5. After you're introduced, thank the person who introduced you, and then greet the audience.

6. Often poetry readings don't offer a microphone, but when they do, it's important for you to know how to adjust the mic so that you're not too close or too far away. Do this quickly, and get right into your reading after you're introduced. Be aware that putting your mouth too close to the mic will create sibilance that you don't want. Avoid asking over and over if your audience can hear you. Once is enough at the very beginning.

7. Introductions for individual poems can be helpful. Although your poems should speak for themselves, a bit of backstory or clarification can warm up your relationship with the audience. Just be sure that you don't talk too much. The audience is there to hear you read your poems, not to hear you talk about them. We've all heard poets whose introductions were longer than their poems. In addition, it's not a good idea to interrupt a poem to tell a story or to assure your audience that the poem is the truth.

8. Read slowly. Allow each word its place in the poem. The inclination to rush is understandable, especially if you're nervous. Relax as much as possible and consciously slow down. Pronounce each word clearly. Above all, don't mumble or let your voice fall away, especially at the end of a poem. Pause and look up at the end of each poem to signal that it's over. Don't rush right to the next poem or begin to chitchat. Let the poem settle.

9. Volume is important. With or without a microphone, try to project your voice to the back of the room. Look at a person seated in the last row, and speak directly to that person.

10. Work on making your voice interesting. The quality of your voice is important. Try using a fuller range than you would in normal conversation. Raise and lower your voice appropriately, but don't go overboard. Be as natural as possible.

11. Make a point of looking up as you read to make sure that you have some level of eye contact with your audience, especially during pauses in the text or at points in the poem where you want special emphasis. A poet who never looks up or who holds written material in front of her face can't be adequately heard. And an audience can't relate to a poet who never looks at them.

12. Avoid saying things like *I just wrote this poem today* or *This is a draft of a poem I'm working on*. Such comments suggest that you're insecure about your work. You never want to give the impression that the audience isn't getting your best work. Apologies almost always reflect poorly on the person giving the reading. Keep in mind that your audience is not waiting for you to mess up—they're hoping you'll be spectacular.

13. Try to stand still unless you have a contextual reason for moving. Typically, moving around at the podium is a symptom of nervousness, and everyone will be aware of it. It's a good idea to consciously plant your feet and straighten your spine. Don't fidget while reading. Sometimes, punctuating certain lines with a movement of your hands is effective, but do not overdo it. You don't want to look as if you're conducting an orchestra.

14. If you trip on a word or flub a line, just keep going. Most of the time the audience won't even notice a slip-up unless you call attention to it. If you lose your place while reading, don't panic. Just pause, find your place, and get on with reading. If you memorize your poems and miss a line, just keep going. The audience won't know that you've left out something.

15. Some audiences applaud after each poem, but some don't. Either way, when you finish a poem, you can signal that it's over with a pause and a smile or a small step back from the mic before moving on to the next piece. If the audience does applaud, be sure to say, *Thank you*. At the end of the reading, after the audience applauds, make a point of final, gracious thanks.

Poem and Prompt

Three Possibilities

1.

To come back to life as another man,
but made of love.

To pack a sandwich and a bag of cherries,
to get on the bus at the first stop,
slide sideways, step to the back,

and wave as we go by
to a boy as he fishes in the River of Time.

Then to ride the bus to the terminus,
the morning light flashing between
badly remembered dreams,
forehead pressed to the cold glass.

2.

Or to return as a locust tree's
smooth seed
kept in the pocket of a boy's favorite jeans.

The boy stands on the bank
of the river, and fishes—
and for his lunch
a sandwich and a bag of cherries.

To be the seed rubbed between
thumb and forefinger,
the sure seed,
made of love, the lucky seed.

3.

Or to return as a single sweet cherry,
bountiful, as I have not been,

whole, as I have not been,
red and rich and round,
as I have not been,

good, as I have not been,
made of love, as I have not been,
with a moon inside, a secret.

Neither to be lost between
possibilities,
nor to be swept along

in the River of Time,
where I am, what I have been.

—Alan Michael Parker

Readers are often intrigued by poems that come in numbered
sections and by the ways a poet connects the sections. Parker
employs a variety of strategies to make connections among the
sections of his poem. First of all, his title lays the groundwork for
the three-section structure.

Parker then uses infinitives to launch the poem and hold together
the sections and the stanzas within the sections. The repetition
of infinitives adds not only structure but also rhythm. Read the
poem aloud and you'll hear its music.

Another strategy Parker uses is contrast. In the first two lines,
the speaker *will come back to life as another man, / but made
of love*. The poet also juxtaposes the serious with the seemingly
trivial. Following the preceding serious line, he gives us *To
pack a sandwich and a bag of cherries*. In section 3, the
speaker contrasts what the cherry is to what he has not been.

The pit inside that cherry is no longer a pit but, in a lovely metaphor, becomes a *moon inside, a secret*.

Another connecting strategy is weaving what's in section 1 into the later sections. The boy seen fishing in section 1 reappears in section 2 with a seed from a locust tree in his pocket. The sandwich and cherries from section 1 become the boy's lunch in section 2. The seed is made of love as the speaker in section 1 hoped to be. A bag of cherries becomes *a single sweet cherry* by the time we get to section 3, an interesting narrowing down of the image. That cherry is *made of love*, looping us back to section 1. And section 1's *River of Time* rolls right along into section 3.

✐ ✐ ✐

Let's take on the challenge of a poem in numbered sections. Let's stick with the number 3 as it's a good symmetrical number. First, think of a category so that you'll immediately have unity of idea, e.g., three excuses, three lies, three injuries, three promises, three indulgences, three reasons for leaving. One idea per section.

To get started, you might employ Parker's strategy of using an infinitive, or you might begin with a word such as *Because, If, When, After,* or *Before*. Whichever beginning you use, return to it repeatedly throughout your poem.

As you move along, use contrast. Be sure to embrace the trivial and contrast it with the serious.

In section 2, bring in your second idea. Weave in some of what's in section 1.

Move to your third idea for section 3. Again, weave in some of what's in the earlier sections, but perhaps narrow down, zoom in.

Like Parker, feel free to vary the number of stanzas per section.

As you revise, work in some of Parker's other techniques, e.g., images that appeal to our senses, repetition, the withholding of the *I* until section 3.

Sample Poems

Three Views of Flight

i.

Gulls plunge toward my raised hands, the undersides
of their wing feathers lined with darkness. One remains
tilted against a neighbor's gabled roof,
one more attached to the near maple's cragged branch, or is it
a leaf, dead and clinging?

ii.

You say the abandoned wasp's nest
reveals nature's drive toward order.
I forgive the swarm, their stinging welts,
but I cannot ease
my panic, their excess
crawling among identical trembling bodies.
I prefer the empty hive
to the pulsing mass, and more,
I prefer the image, a painting shaded
boldly enough to convey its art's artifice.

iii.

Through jagged slats, the sky
soars. Nothing
floats or falls, dives toward me or away.
My vision fills, a bare
hayloft, dust motes, the barn's collapsing
roof, the blue, the blue.

—Lynn Domina
published in *Dunes Review*

Three Lives

1.

To enter marriage at twenty, old enough
and yet too young, too young.

Old enough to cook mushrooms and peas
to mix into rice, too young to understand
the landlady downstairs is dying, even
as she feeds raw hamburger to the spaniel
nesting on her lap.

And oh the joy of listening to curfew bells
chiming across the river, delighted to be
out of the confines of dormitory life.

Old enough to bring a baby boy
home to a used crib in the living room
after twenty hours hard labor.

2.

To finally decide to divorce, after
the first house, years of holiday meals,
barbecues, two children, and a series
of dogs—the one that chewed the
window frames left behind.

After predictable chimes from the alarm
meaning time to get up for another day,
escaping the confines of four walls, one
closet with both his and her clothes.

Old enough to know the sorrow of losing
what might have been, yet still too young
to know the gift of looking back with
forgiveness, another kind of love.

3.

To dare to love again, marry again—
so many lives we leave behind—
now cooking vegetarian, sharing the
daily red pot of tea, driving nights to
lofts in Manhattan where poems chime.

Still too young to believe death
is moving closer, cancer a promise
on the horizon, and then, and then—

in the ICU after savoring lemon sorbet
melting on his tongue, he gives me his
wedding ring, makes his peace with our
goodbye, dies while I sing *Amazing Grace,*

and I am old enough to know this incantation
is a newborn child I bring home to myself.

—Penny Harter

Top Tips: Finding Your Book

—Alberto Rios

The following are some useful ways of thinking about manuscript organization, with the intent of letting your book show itself to you. Try all of these, and listen carefully each time to what the newly gathered manuscript has to say.

1. Temporal Narrative suggests time as your editor. This is an old, but often effective, approach. Time orders things in an often unexpected but logical way. Temporal narrative might be the order in which the poems were written, the age of the speaker, or temporal indicators within the poems themselves.

2. Backward Temporal Narrative can also be effective. If you walk along a hiking trail one way and see certain things, returning along that trail ought to be equally coherent and connected, with the same view of things, but new.

> *When you start with a portrait and search for a pure form, a clear volume, through successive eliminations, you arrive inevitably at the egg. Likewise, starting with the egg and following the same process in reverse, one finishes with the portrait.*—Pablo Picasso

3. Nature can be an organizing schema. You might group your poems by season or elements, literally or metaphorically. Poems about fall, for example, would include anything that drops or expends energy. Winter poems would include anything about dormancy.

4. Organic approaches are based on the physical qualities of the items described. For example, a book of love poems might be organized by head, neck, clavicle, chest, and, uh, toes.

5. Link by Colors, by Smells. We're talking about the senses here, but be loose or open in your sensibility. Include a poem with a red object in it, even—and especially—if the word *red* does not come up in the poem, and pair it with another poem containing something else that is red in it. Link poems or sections by smells, by tastes, by senses we haven't even discovered yet.

6. Orchestrated Structures link dissimilar ideas that share a single characteristic. Rather than linking all the poems about ice cream, for example, this might simply be the joining of a group of poems about Antarctica, the last look of a partner you've just broken up with, the broken ice maker in your refrigerator, and songs about Christmas. The connection is clear—cold—but the circumstances are not at all necessarily joined.

7. Logical Sequence involves identifying what a reader needs to know in order to understand the next thing, then ordering the poems so that they make sense. This is like climbing a ladder.

8. Spiral Structures are chains of associations based on similarity. The spiral should be like a hawk circling slowly in and down. In the spiral structure one line speaks to another in a long chain; the movement is not circular and closed but slowly and evenly forward.

> We shall not cease from exploration / And the end of all our exploring / Will be to arrive where we started / And know the place for the first time.—T. S. Eliot

9. Mosaic structuring uses many small fragments to tell a larger story. Like a mosaic, the individual poems are bits of color and shape. From a distance, as the reader stands back and puts them all together, a picture emerges. A mystery is well-served by this form, though the process serves many kinds of manuscripts. The test of this form is, of course, that something clear must emerge.

10. Objective Ordering may be appropriate depending on the subject of the manuscript. If the book is about the anonymity of force, you might want to use untitled poems identified by only number. You might alphabetize the poems by the first word. You might throw the poems up into the air and order them according to the whim of their landing. Objectivity, if you can truly live with it, suggests a sense of metaphysics— that something out there, rather than us, is in control—or the more troubling suggestion of what has been called *pataphysics*—that neither we nor anything else out there is in control. Getting a reader to understand this, however, might take an author's note.

11. Alphabetizing is a strong but deceptive organizer, both whimsical and efficient at the same time—while being neither finally. It simply offers an effective foundation for letting the manuscript speak for itself. Related to Objective Ordering, it is an institutionalized version of throwing your poems up in the air and letting the order settle itself. The trouble, of course, with these methods is that you will not be able to stick with them. Something will trouble you, or you will want to just exchange one poem for another in the order. Examine this feeling. The ordering sensibility you are looking for may be resident in your inability to truly let objectivity order the manuscript.

12. Eccentric Structures involve oddities or non sequitur thinking linked together by virtue of their lack of connection. Surrealism made a mighty attempt at this and succeeded in large measure by finding value in what would seem at first meaningless and nonsensical. Psychotherapy often plays in this garden as well.

13. Last-line-First-line Dialogue is the most whimsical and often the most fun. See what the last line of a poem would connect to in the first line of another poem. This will establish a dialogue among the poems in the book. Even though you may also realistically need to consider the second line and the second-to-last line, the idea is to forget about the body of the poem and just look at what the first and last lines have to say to one another. This creates a coherent book in its in-between spaces, and gives a surprising sense of motion or connection in the moment—that is, connection where we do not expect to find it.

14. The Old Neighborhood is still something to count on, an indestructible, definable, visceral, and tangible home-ness. I am talking here about place, which—if you know something about one—you ought to consider. Geography is a natural connector, and an exasperating separator.

Bonus Prompt: The Instruction Poem

Write down the steps involved in doing something you know how to do.

Some possibilities:

> How to plant tulips
> How to make meatloaf
> How to wash a dog or a child
> How to repair a broken chair, plate, marriage, child
> How to keep squirrels away from the bird feeder

Draft a poem using the steps in your list. Write quickly, letting the poem take you where it will.

The goal, of course, is to let the poem rise above and beyond the instructions. Keep writing until that happens.

Contributors

Christopher Bakken is the author of three books of poetry, most recently *Eternity & Oranges* (U of Pittsburgh, 2016). He serves as Director of Writing Workshops in Greece and is Frederick F. Seely Professor of English at Allegheny College.

Ellen Bass is the author of three poetry books, most recently *Like a Beggar* (Copper Canyon, 2016). Her awards include the New Letters Poetry Prize, three Pushcart Prizes, and fellowships from the California Arts Council and the NEA. She teaches in the low-residency MFA program at Pacific University.

Andrea Bates has published two chapbooks of poetry, *Origami Heart* and *The Graveyard Sonnets*. Her writing has appeared in *Baltimore Review, Cutthroat, Quiddity,* and elsewhere.

Joseph Bathanti is the former Poet Laureate of North Carolina (2012-14) and the author of ten books, including *The 13th Sunday after Pentecost* (LSU, 2016). Recipient of the 2016 North Carolina Award for Literature, he is the McFarlane Family Distinguished Professor of Interdisciplinary Education at Appalachian State University.

Jan Beatty is the author of five poetry books, most recently *Jackknife* (U of Pittsburgh, 2018). Her awards include the 1994 Agnes Lynch Starrett Prize, the Pablo Neruda Prize for Poetry, and two fellowships from the Pennsylvania Council on the Arts. She is director of the creative writing program at Carlow University.

Jeanne Marie Beaumont is the author of four collections of poetry, most recently *Letters from Limbo* (CavanKerry, 2016). She has taught at Rutgers University, The Frost Place, and the Unterberg Poetry Center of the 92nd St. Y.

Roy Beckemeyer is the author of *Amanuensis Angel* (Spartan, 2018) and *Stage Whispers* (Meadowlark, 2018). His first book won a Kansas Notable Book Award. He is a retired engineer and scientific journal editor.

Libby Bernardin is the author of *Stones Ripe for Sowing* (Press 53, 2018) and two chapbooks. Her publication credits include *Southern Poetry Review, Asheville Poetry Review,* and *Notre Dame Review.* She is a past recipient of the SC Poetry Society Forum Prize and the NC Poetry of Witness Award.

George Bilgere has published seven collections of poetry, most recently *Blood Pages* (U of Pittsburgh, 2018). He is the recipient of a Pushcart Prize and grants from the Witter Bynner Foundation, the NEA, the Fulbright Commission, and the Ohio Arts Council. He teaches creative writing at John Carroll University.

Adrian Blevins is the author of three collections of poetry, most recently *Appalachians Run Amok* (Two Sylvias, 2018), which won the Wilder Prize. Her first collection, *The Brass Girl Brouhaha* (Ausable, 2003), won the Kate Tufts Discovery Award.

Elizabeth Bodien is the author of *Blood, Metal, Fiber, Rock* (Kelsay, 2018). Her work has appeared in such publications as *Cimarron Review*, *The Fourth River*, and *Schuylkill Valley Journal*.

Jody Bolz is the author of three poetry collections, most recently *The Near and Far* (Turning Point, 2019). Among her honors are a Rona Jaffe Foundation writer's award and a grant from the Maryland State Arts Council. She edits the journal *Poet Lore*.

Bob Bradshaw is a retired programmer living in California. His poems are included in both volumes of *The Crafty Poet: A Portable Workshop* and have been published in such journals as *Apple Valley Review, Eclectica,* and *Pedestal Magazine*.

Nancy Susanna Breen is the author of two chapbooks, including *Rites and Observances* (Finishing Line, 2004). Her journal and anthology publications include *Encore* and *The Book of Donuts*. She is the former editor of *Poet's Market*.

Traci Brimhall is the author of three collections of poetry, most recently *Saudade* (Copper Canyon, 2017). Her poems have appeared in such journals as *Poetry, Ploughshares,* and *Kenyon Review*. The recipient of a 2013 NEA fellowship, she teaches at Kansas State University.

Sharon Bryan is the author of four books of poems, most recently *Sharp Stars* (BOA, 2009). Her awards include two NEA fellowships, the Isabella Gardner Award for *Sharp Stars,* and an Artist's Trust grant from the Washington State Arts Council. She teaches in the low-residency MFA in Creative Writing Program at Lesley University.

Lauren Camp is the author of three books, most recently *One Hundred Hungers* (Tupelo, 2016), which won the Dorset Prize. Her poems have appeared in *Boston Review, Beloit Poetry Journal,* and the *Poem-a-Day* series from The Academy of American Poets.

Roger Camp is a photographer, educator, and poet whose work has appeared in *Poetry East, North American Review, Southern Poetry Review,* and elsewhere. He is professor emeritus from Golden West College where he taught photography.

Luanne Castle is the author of *Doll God* (Aldrich Press), which received the 2015 New Mexico-Arizona Book Award. Her work has appeared in *Copper Nickel, River Teeth,* and elsewhere. She has been a Fellow at the Center for Ideas and Society in California.

Richard Cecil is the author of four collections of poems, including *Twenty-First Century Blues* (Crab Orchard, 2004). His poems have appeared in such journals as *Poetry, The Georgia Review,* and *Virginia Quarterly Review.* He teaches in the Hutton Honors College of Indiana University.

Nicole Cooley is the author of five books of poetry, most recently *Girl after Girl after Girl* (LSU, 2017). Her awards include The Walt Whitman Award, an NEA fellowship, and the Emily Dickinson Award. She is the director of the MFA Program in Creative Writing and Literary Translation at Queens College-CUNY.

Gail Comorat is the author of *Phases of the Moon* (Finishing Line). Her work has appeared in *Gargoyle, Grist,* and *The Widows' Handbook.* She has received two poetry fellowships from the Delaware Division of the Arts and was the 2012 winner of the Artsmith Literary Award.

Meg Day is the author of *Last Psalm at Sea Level* (Barrow Street, 2014), winner of the Barrow Street Book Prize and a finalist for the 2016 Kate Tufts Discovery Award. Her awards include the Amy Lowell Traveling Scholarship and an NEA fellowship. She is an Assistant Professor of English & Creative Writing at Franklin & Marshall College.

Jessica de Koninck is the author of one full-length collection, *Cutting Room* (Terrapin Books, 2016), and one chapbook, *Repairs* (Finishing Line). Her poems have appeared in *Eclectica Magazine, Mom Egg Review, Verse Daily,* and elsewhere. She serves on the *Jewish Currents* editorial board.

Oliver de la Paz is the author of five books of poetry, most recently *Labyrinths* (U. of Akron, 2019). Recipient of a New York Foundation Fellowship, he co-chairs the advisory board of Kundiman and serves on the AWP's Board of Trustees. He teaches at Holy Cross.

Maggie Dietz is the author of two poetry collections, most recently *That Kind of Happy* (U of Chicago, 2016). Her honors include the Jane Kenyon Award, Grolier Poetry Prize, and fellowships from the New Hampshire State Council on the Arts and the Fine Arts Work Center. She teaches at the University of Massachusetts Lowell.

Emari DiGiorgio is the author of two collections, most recently *Girl Torpedo* (Agape, 2018). Her awards include the Elinor Benedict Poetry Prize and a poetry fellowship from the New Jersey State Council on the Arts. She teaches at Stockton University.

Lynn Domina is the author of two collections of poetry, most recently *Framed in Silence* (Main Street Rag, 2011), and the editor of a collection of essays, *Poets on the Psalms*. She serves as Head of the English Department at Northern Michigan University.

Patrick Donnelly is the author of four books of poetry, including *Nocturnes of the Brothel of Ruin* (Four Way Books), a 2013 finalist for the Lambda Literary Award. His poems have appeared in such journals as *The Yale Review, American Poetry Review,* and *Ploughshares*. He is director of the Poetry Seminar at The Frost Place.

Camille T. Dungy is the author of four collections of poetry, most recently *Trophic Cascade* (Wesleyan, 2017). She is the recipient of fellowships and grants from the NEA, The Sustainable Arts Foundation, and the Diane Middlebrook Residency Fellowship. She teaches at Colorado State University.

Peter Everwine has published seven collections of poetry, including *Listening Long and Late* (U of Pittsburgh, 2013). He is the recipient of a Pushcart Prize, an NEA fellowship, and a Guggenheim fellowship.

Patricia Fargnoli is the author of five books, most recently *Hallowed: New & Selected Poems* (Tupelo, 2017). Her awards include the May Swenson Award, NH Literary Award, and Sheila Mooton Poetry Book Award. She served as the New Hampshire Poet Laureate from 2006-2009.

Ann Fisher-Wirth is the author of five poetry collections, most recently *Mississippi* (Wings, 2018). Recipient of two Mississippi Arts Commission poetry awards she teaches at the University of Mississippi, where she also directs the Environmental Studies program.

Chris Forhan is the author of three poetry books, most recently *Black Leapt In*, winner of the 2009 Barrow Street Book Prize. He has received an NEA fellowship and two Pushcart Prizes. He teaches at Butler University.

Vievee Francis is the author of three books of poetry, most recently *Forest Primeval* (Northwestern UP, 2016), which received the 2016 Hurston Wright Legacy Award and the 2017 Kingsley Tufts Poetry Award. She teaches at Dartmouth College.

Jeannine Hall Gailey is the author of five books of poetry, most recently *Field Guide to the End of the World,* winner of the 2015 Moon City Press Book. Her work has appeared in such journals as *American Poetry Review, Notre Dame Review,* and *Prairie Schooner.*

James Galvin has published eight books of poems, most recently *Everything We Always Knew Was True* (Copper Canyon, 2016). His honors include a Lila Wallace-Reader's Digest Writers' Award, a Lannan Literary Award, and fellowships from the Guggenheim Foundation, the Ingram Merrill Foundation, and the NEA.

Gaye Gambell-Peterson is the author of two chapbooks, *pale leaf floating* (Midwest Women Poets Series) and *MYnd mAp*. Her poems have been published in *American Journal of Poetry, Erase/Transform,* and *Flood Stage: An Anthology of St. Louis.*

Megan Gannon is the author of *Cumberland*, a novel, and *White Nightgown*, a collection of poems. Her work appears in *Barrow Street, Boulevard,* and *Crazyhorse*. She is an Assistant Professor of English at Ripon College in Wisconsin.

Deborah Gerrish is the author of three collections of poems, most recently *Light in Light* (Resource Publications, 2017). Her poems have appeared in *Lips, Paterson Literary Review,* and *The Crafty Poet II*. She teaches poetry at Fairleigh Dickinson University.

Jennifer Givhan is the author of three poetry collections, most recently *Girl with Death Mask* (Blue Light, 2018). Her honors include an NEA Fellowship, a PEN/Rosenthal Emerging Voices Fellowship, and The Frost Place Latin@ Scholarship.

Patricia L. Goodman is the author of two poetry books, most recently *Walking with Scissors* (Kelsay, 2019). Her work has also been published in *Wild Goose Poetry Review, The Crafty Poet II,* and elsewhere. She teaches poetry in the Osher Lifelong Learning program.

Juliana Gray is the author of three poetry books, most recently *Honeymoon Palsy* (Measure, 2017), as well as the chapbook *Anne Boleyn's Sleeve* (Winged City, 2013). She teaches at Alfred University.

William Greenfield is the author of a chapbook, *Momma's Boy Gone Bad* (Finishing Line, 2017). His poems have been published in such journals as *The Westchester Review, Carve Magazine*, and *Tar River Poetry*.

Susan Gundlach's poetry has appeared in such journals as *After Hours* and **82 Review*. Her children's poems have appeared in *Cricket* magazine and *Balloons Lit Journal*. She is co-editor of the poetry anthology *In Plein Air*.

Barbara Hamby is the author of several poetry collections, most recently *Bird Odyssey* (U of Pittsburgh, 2018). She has won the Vassar Miller Prize, Kate Tufts Discovery Award, and fellowships from the Guggenheim Foundation and the NEA. In 2010 she was named a Distinguished University Scholar at Florida State University.

Penny Harter's books include *The Night Marsh*. Her work has appeared in such journals as *Persimmon, Rattle*, and *Tiferet*. She has won three fellowships from the New Jersey State Council on the Arts and the Mary Carolyn Davies Award from the PSA.

Hunt Hawkins is the author of *The Domestic Life,* which received the Agnes Lynch Starret Poetry Prize. His poems have appeared in *The Georgia Review*, *Poetry*, *TriQuarterly,* and elsewhere. He teaches at the University of South Florida.

Shayla Hawkins is the author of *Carambola* (David Robert, 2012). She is a Cave Canem Fellow and has been a featured reader at the Dodge Poetry Festival and the Library of Congress. Her work has been published in *Windsor Review, Bonsai,* and elsewhere.

Cynthia Marie Hoffman is the author of three books of poetry, most recently *Call Me When You Want to Talk about the Tombstones* (Persea, 2018). Her awards include a Diane Middlebrook Fellowship and an Individual Artist Fellowship from the Wisconsin Arts Board.

Karen Paul Holmes is the author of two full-length poetry books, most recently *No Such Thing as Distance* (Terrapin, 2018). Named a 2016 Best Emerging Poet by Stay Thirsty Media, she has published poems in *Prairie Schooner, Crab Orchard Review,* and *Poet Lore*.

Jenny Hubbard is the author of two novels, *And We Stay* and *Paper Covers Rock,* both of which earned top honors from the American Library Association. She is the writer-in-residence at Woodberry Forest School in Virginia.

Tina Kelley is the author of three poetry collections, most recently *Abloom and Awry* (CavanKerry, 2017). Her first collection, *The Gospel of Galore,* won a 2003 Washington State Book Award, and her chapbook, *Ardor,* won the 2017 Jacar Press competition.

Sheila Kelly has been published in such journals as *Paterson Literary Review* and *Intima: A Journal of Narrative Medicine*. A retired psychotherapist, she leads writing workshops in the University of Pittsburgh's Osher Lifelong Learning Institute.

Adele Kenny is the author of several poetry books, most recently *A Lightness, A Thirst, or Nothing at All* (Welcome Rain, 2015). Her awards include two poetry fellowships from the NJ State Council on the Arts and Kean University's Distinguished Alumni Award. She is founding director of the Carriage House Poetry Series.

David Kirby is the author of more than two dozen volumes of criticism, essays, children's literature, pedagogy, and poetry. His awards include fellowships from the Guggenheim Foundation and the NEA, as well as several Pushcart Prizes. In 2016 he won the Florida Humanities Council's Lifetime Achievement Award for Writing.

Kim Klugh is a poet and freelance contributor for *Business Woman* magazine. Her poems appear in *The Crafty Poet II: A Portable Workshop* and in *Sunday*, a magazine supplement.

Jennifer Kosuda studied psychology and has an MA in Teaching. She teaches English Language Arts and Special Education in NJ.

Dorianne Laux is the author of six books of poetry, most recently *Only as the Day Is Long: New and Selected Poems* (W. W. Norton, 2019). Her awards include a Pushcart Prize, two fellowships from the NEA, and a Guggenheim Fellowship. She teaches poetry at North Carolina State University.

Ada Limón is the author of five books of poetry, most recently *The Carrying* (Milkweed, 2018). She is also the author of *Bright Dead Things*, a finalist for the 2015 National Book Award in Poetry, the Kingsley Tufts Poetry Award, and the National Book Critics Circle Award.

Nancy Chen Long is the author of *Light into Bodies,* which won the 2016 Tampa Review Prize for Poetry. She received a 2017 NEA fellowship and has had work in *The Southern Review, Pleiades*, and *Alaska Quarterly Review.*

Sandy Longhorn is the author of three poetry books, most recently *The Alchemy of My Mortal Form* (Trio House, 2015), which won the 2014 Louise Bogan Award. She teaches in the MFA program at the University of Central Arkansas, directs the C. D. Wright Women Writers Conference, and co-edits the journal *Heron Tree*.

Thomas Lux was the author of fourteen books of poetry. Until his death in 2017, he served as the Bourne Professor of Poetry and the director of the McEver Visiting Writers Program at the Georgia Institute of Technology. His honors included the Kingsley Tufts Poetry Award, a Guggenheim fellowship, and three NEA fellowships.

Anne Marie Macari is the author of four poetry books, most recently *Red Deer* (Persea, 2015). Her first book, *Ivory Cradle* (Copper Canyon, 2000) won the APR/Honickman First Book Prize in Poetry. She founded and teaches in the Drew MFA Program for Poetry & Poetry in Translation.

Ted Mathys is the author of *Null Set* (Coffee House, 2015) and three previous books of poetry. He has earned fellowships and awards from the NEA, New York Foundation for the Arts, and PSA, and his work has appeared in *American Poetry Review, Boston Review,* and elsewhere.

Joan Mazza is the author of six books, including *Dreaming Your Real Self* (Penguin/Putnam). Her poetry has appeared in *Rattle, The MacGuffin,* and *The Nation.*

Campbell McGrath is the author of ten collections of poetry, most recently *XX: Poems for the Twentieth Century* (Ecco Press, 2016). His honors include the Kingsley Tufts Poetry Award, a MacArthur Foundation Genius Grant, and a Guggenheim fellowship.

Jennifer Militello is the author of three poetry books, most recently *A Camouflage of Specimens and Garments* (Tupelo, 2016). Her book, *Flinch of Song*, received the Tupelo Press First Book Award. She teaches in the MFA program at New England College.

Judith Montgomery is the author of two books, most recently *Litany for Wound and Bloom* (Uttered Chaos, 2018). Her poems have appeared in *Prairie Schooner, Rattle,* and elsewhere. Her awards include fellowships from Literary Arts and the Oregon Arts Commission.

John Murillo's first poetry collection, *Up Jump the Boogie* (Cypher, 2010), was a finalist for the 2011 Kate Tufts Discovery Award. His honors include a Pushcart Prize, two Larry Neal Writers Awards, and fellowships from the NEA and Cave Canem Foundation.

Peter E. Murphy is the author of eight books and chapbooks. His work has appeared in *Beloit Poetry Journal, Hayden's Ferry Review, The Literary Review,* and elsewhere. He is the founder of Murphy Writing of Stockton University which sponsors the Winter Poetry & Prose Getaway.

Kathy Nelson is the author of two chapbooks, most recently *Whose Names Have Slipped Away* (Finishing Line, 2016). Her work has appeared in *Asheville Poetry Review, Tar River Poetry,* and elsewhere.

Camille Norvaisas is the author of *Rare as the Kotuku* (Aldrich, 2015). Her journal publications include *Schuylkill Valley Journal, Off the Coast,* and the *American Journal of Nursing*.

Rebecca Hart Olander has had poems published in *Mom Egg Review,* the *Plath Poetry Project,* and *Solstice*. She is a past winner of the Women's National Book Association poetry contest. She is the editor/director of Perugia Press .

April Ossmann is the author of two poetry books, most recently *Event Boundaries* (Four Way, 2018). She is the recipient of a 2013 Vermont Arts Council Creation Grant and a *Prairie Schooner* Readers' Choice Award. She is a faculty editor for the low-residency MFA in Creative Writing Program at Sierra Nevada College.

Alan Michael Parker is the author of eight collections of poems, most recently *The Ladder* (Tupelo, 2016), which received the 2017 Brockman-Campbell Award. His honors include three Pushcart Prizes, two appearances in *The Best American Poetry,* and the Fineline Prize.

Linda Parsons is the author of four poetry collections, her latest *This Shaky Earth* (Texas Review, 2016). She is the reviews editor at *Pine Mountain Sand & Gravel* and has contributed to *The Georgia Review, Iowa Review, Prairie Schooner,* and elsewhere.

Molly Peacock is the author of six books of poetry, most recently *The Analyst* (W. W. Norton, 2017). She is Series Editor of *The Best Canadian Poetry* and has published in such journals as *Poetry, Malahat Review,* and *The Yale Review*. She has received awards from the Ingram Merrill Foundation, Woodrow Wilson Foundation, and NEA.

Marge Piercy has published nineteen volumes of poetry, most recently *Made in Detroit* (Knopf, 2015). She has also written novels, plays, several volumes of nonfiction, and a memoir. She is the recipient of four honorary doctorates.

Lawrence Raab is the author of nine collections, most recently *The Life Beside This One* (Tupelo, 2017). His book, *Mistaking Each Other for Ghosts* (Tupelo, 2015), was longlisted for the National Book Award.

Emily Ransdell's poems have appeared in *Poet Lore, Tar River Poetry, American Life in Poetry*, and elsewhere. She has been a finalist for the Rattle Poetry Prize and the Janet B. McCabe Prize.

Chelsea Rathburn is the author of three collections, most recently *Still Life with Mother & Knife* (LSU, 2019). Her poems have appeared in *Poetry, Ploughshares,* and elsewhere. She is an assistant professor at Young Harris College, where she directs the creative writing program.

Anjela Villarreal Ratliff, a retired educator, has published poems and photographs in literary journals and anthologies, including *Pilgrimage, San Pedro River Review,* and *The Book of Donuts.*

Susanna Rich is the author of three poetry books, most recently *Surfing for Jesus*. She has been an Emmy Award nominee, Fulbright Fellow in Creative Writing, and recipient of the Presidential Excellence Award for Distinguished Teaching at Kean University.

Susan Rich is the author of four books, most recently *Cloud Pharmacy* (White Pine, 2014). Her poems have won awards from PEN USA and the Fulbright Foundation, and have appeared in such journals as *Alaska Quarterly Review, Harvard Review*, and *The Southern Review.*

Jenna Rindo has had work published in such journals as *Natural Bridge, Tampa Review*, and *Bellingham Review*. She won first place in the 2018 Wisconsin People & Ideas Poetry Contest. A former pediatric nurse, she now teaches English to non-native speakers.

Alberto Rios served as the inaugural Poet Laureate of Arizona, 2013-2015. He is the author of thirteen books of poetry and prose, most recently *A Small Story about the Sky* (Copper Canyon, 2015). He is a recipient of fellowships from the Guggenheim Foundation and the NEA and has received six Pushcart Prizes and the Walt Whitman Award.

Elizabeth Lindsey Rogers is the author of *Chord Box* (U of Arkansas, 2013). Her poems and essays have appeared in *Field, Crazyhorse, Prairie Schooner*, and elsewhere.

Pattiann Rogers has published thirteen books of poetry, most recently *Quickening Fields* (Penguin, 2017). Her awards include the Burroughs Medal for Lifetime Achievement in Nature Poetry, two NEA fellowships, a Guggenheim fellowship, and five Pushcart Prizes.

Kenneth Ronkowitz's poetry appears in *The Crafty Poet* and in such journals as the *English Journal, Tiferet,* and the *Paterson Literary Review*. He has edited Poets Online since 1998 and teaches at NJIT.

Natasha Sajé is the author of three books of poems, most recently *Vivarium* (Tupelo, 2014), and a poetry handbook, *Windows and Doors: A Poet Reads Literary Theory* (Michigan, 2014). Her honors include a Fulbright fellowship and the Utah Book Award.

Christopher Salerno is the author of four books, most recently *Sun & Urn,* which received the Georgia Poetry Prize (U of Georgia, 2017). Recipient of a NJ State Council on the Arts poetry fellowship, he teaches at William Paterson University and is the editor of Saturnalia Books.

Jennifer Saunders is the author of *Self-Portrait with Housewife,* winner of the 2017 Clockwise Chapbook Competition from Tebot Bach Press. Her work has appeared in *Glass, Spillway,* and elsewhere. She teaches skating in a hockey school and lives in Switzerland.

Penelope Scambly Schott is the author of several poetry books, most recently *House of the Cardamom Seed* (Cherry Grove, 2018). Her awards include the Oregon Book Award for Poetry, Sarah Lantz Memorial Award, and Orphic Poetry Prize.

Carla Schwartz is the author of two full-length poetry collections, most recently *Intimacy with the Wind* (Finishing Line, 2017). Her poems have appeared in *Aurorean, Mom Egg Review, Solstice,* and elsewhere.

Carol Seitchik is the author of a chapbook, *The Distance from Odessa.* Her poems have been published in *A Feast of Cape Ann Poets* and *Mom Egg Review.* She works as a visual arts curator.

Danielle Sellers is the author of two poetry books, most recently *The Minor Territories* (Sundress, 2018). Her poems have appeared in *Prairie Schooner, Cimarron Review, Poet Lore,* and elsewhere.

Diane Seuss is the author of four books, most recently *Still Life with Two Dead Peacocks and a Girl* (Graywolf, 2018). Her earlier book, *Four-Legged Girl,* was a finalist for the Pulitzer Prize. She has published in such journals as *Poetry, The Iowa Review,* and *The New Yorker.*

Betsy Sholl is the author of nine books of poetry, most recently *House of Sparrows: New and Selected Poems* (Wisconsin Poetry Series, 2018). A founding member of Alice James Books, she teaches in the MFA program at Vermont College of Fine Arts. She served as Poet Laureate of Maine from 2006 to 2011.

Martha Silano is the author of five poetry collections, most recently *Gravity Assist* (Saturnalia, 2019). Her poems have been featured on *Poetry Daily* and published in *Poetry, New England Review, American Poetry Review*, and elsewhere.

Dianne Silvestri is author of the chapbook, *Necessary Sentiments.* Her poems have appeared in *Naugatuck River Review, Barrow Street*, and *Zingara Poetry Review.* She worked as a teaching physician until disabled by illness. She copy-edits the journal *Dermatitis.*

Linda Simone is the author of *The River Will Save Us* (Aldrich, 2018) and two chapbooks. Her poems have appeared in *Indiana Voice Journal* and *Carnival.* She was among thirty poets selected for San Antonio's 2018 Tricentennial chapbook.

Maggie Smith is the author of three books of poetry, most recently *Good Bones* (Tupelo, 2017). *The Well Speaks of Its Own Poison* (Tupelo, 2015) received the Dorset Prize. She is the recipient of six Individual Excellence Awards from the Ohio Arts Council and fellowships from the Sustainable Arts Foundation and the NEA.

Patricia Smith is the author of eight books, including *Incendiary Art* (Triquarterly, 2017), winner of the 2018 Kingsley Tufts Poetry Award, 2017 Los Angeles Times Book Prize, 2018 NAACP Image Award, and finalist for the 2018 Pulitzer Prize. Other honors include a Guggenheim fellowship, an NEA fellowship, and two Pushcart Prizes.

Mark Smith-Soto has authored three chapbooks and three full-length poetry collections, most recently *Time Pieces* (Main Street Rag, 2015). His work, recognized in 2006 with an NEA fellowship, has appeared in *Antioch Review, Kenyon Review, Nimrod*, and elsewhere.

Maxine Susman is the author of six chapbooks, most recently *Provincelands* (Finishing Line, 2016). She teaches writing at the Osher Lifelong Learning Institute of Rutgers University, where she earned the Marlene Pomper Teaching Award.

Lee Upton is the author of five books of poetry, most recently *Bottle the Bottles the Bottles the Bottles* (Cleveland State, 2015). She is also the author of a book of short stories and a book of creative nonfiction. Her awards include the Lyric Poetry Award, a Pushcart Prize, and the National Poetry Series Award.

Denise Utt has published poetry in the *Bellevue Literary Review, Paterson Literary Review*, and other journals. Her work has also appeared in the *Forgotten Women Anthology.*

Sidney Wade is the author of seven poetry books, most recently *Bird Book* (Atelier26, 2017). Her poems have appeared in *The New Yorker, Poetry,* and elsewhere. She has served as President of AWP and is professor emerita at the University of Florida.

Scott Wiggerman is the author of three books of poetry, most recently *Leaf and Beak: Sonnets,* finalist for the Helen C. Smith Memorial Award. He is also the co-editor of *Wingbeats I & II: Exercises & Practice in Poetry* (Dos Gatos).

Robert Wrigley is the author of ten poetry collections, most recently *Box* (Penguin, 2017). His honors include fellowships from the NEA, the Idaho State Commission on the Arts, and the Guggenheim Foundation, as well as the Frederick Bock Prize, the Theodore Roethke Award, and two Pushcart Prizes.

Lisa Young is the author of the poetry collection, *When the Earth* (Quattro Books), and a chapbook. Her work has been published in *Minola Review,* the *Maple Tree Literary Supplement*, and elsewhere. She is founding editor of *Juniper: A Poetry Journal.*

Credits

Christopher Bakken. "Driving the Beast." Copyright © 2017 by Christopher Bakken. First published in *Poem-a-Day*/Academy of American Poets. Reprinted by permission of the author.

Joseph Bathanti. "Emerson Street" from *The 13th Sunday after Pentecost* (LSU P). Copyright © 2016 by Joseph Bathanti. Reprinted by permission of the author.

Jeanne Marie Beaumont. "Portrait with Closed Eyes" from *Letters from Limbo* (CavanKerry Press). Copyright © 2016 by Jeanne Marie Beaumont. Reprinted by permission of the author.

Jody Bolz. "Repairs." Copyright © 2016 by Jody Bolz. First published in *Southern Poetry Review*. Reprinted by permission of the author.

Roger Camp. "Baby on a Train." Copyright © 2016 by Roger Camp. First published in *Southern Poetry Review*. Reprinted by permission of the author.

Richard Cecil. "Fantastic Voyage." Copyright © 2016 by Richard Cecil. First published in *The Cincinnati Review*. Reprinted by permission of the author.

Emari DiGiorgio. "Pediatrics" from *The Things a Body Might Become* (Five Oaks Press). Copyright © 2017 by Emari DiGiorgio. Reprinted by permission of the author.

Maggie Dietz. "April Lamentation" from *That Kind of Happy* (Univ of Chicago). Copyright © 2016 by Maggie Dietz. Reprinted by permission of the author.

Camille T. Dungy. "Because it looked hotter that way" from *Trophic Cascade* (Wesleyan University Press). Copyright © 2017 by Camille T. Dungy. Used by permission from Wesleyan University Press.

Peter Everwine. "The Day." Copyright © 2016 by Peter Everwine. First published in *New Letters*. Reprinted by permission of the author.

Vievee Francis. "Epicurean" from *Forest Primeval* (Northwestern University Press). Copyright © 2015. Reprinted by permission of the author.

James Galvin. "On the Sadness of Wedding Dresses" from *Everything We Always Knew Was True* (Copper Canyon Press). Copyright © 2016 by James Galvin. Reprinted by permission of the author.

Jeannine Hall Gailey. "But It Was an Accident" from *Field Guide to the End of the World* (Moon City Press). Copyright © 2016 by Jeannine Hall Gailey. Reprinted by permission of the author.

Juliana Gray. "Maraschino" from *Honeymoon Palsy* (Measure Press). Copyright © 2017 by Juliana Gray. Reprinted by permission of the author.

William Greenfield. "Five to Ten." Copyright © 2017 by William Greenfield. First published in *Tar River Poetry*. Reprinted by permission of the author.

Hunt Hawkins. "When Sex Was Kissing." Copyright © 2017 by Hunt Hawkins. First published in *Poet Lore*. Reprinted by permission of the author.

Bob Hicok. "Elegy's" from *Elegy Owed*. Copyright © 2013 by Bob Hicok. Reprinted with the permission of The Permissions Company, Inc., on behalf of Copper Canyon Press.

Kimberly Johnson. "Blanks" from *Uncommon Prayer* (Persea Books). Copyright © 2014 by Kimberly Johnson. Reprinted by permission of the author.

Ada Limón. "Downhearted" from *Bright Dead Things* (Milkweed Editions). Copyright © 2015 by Ada Limón. Reprinted with permission from Milkweed Editions.

Nancy Chen Long. "What Some Things Are Worth According to Her Grandfather" from *Light into Bodies* (U of Tampa Press). Copyright © 2017 by Nancy Chen Long. Reprinted by permission of University of Tampa Press.

Thomas Lux. "The Joy-Bringer" from *God Particles: Poems by Thomas Lux*. Copyright © 2008 by Thomas Lux. Reprinted by permission of Houghton Mifflin Harcourt Publishing Company. All rights reserved.

Ted Mathys. "Apostrophe to S." Copyright © 2017 by Ted Mathys. First published in *The Georgia Review*. Reprinted by permission of the author.

John Murillo. "Variations on a Theme by Elizabeth Bishop." Copyright © 2015 by John Murillo. First published in *Prairie Schooner*. Reprinted by permission of the author.

April Ossmann. "Thinking Like an Editor: How to Order Your Poetry Manuscript." Copyright © 2011 by April Ossmann. First published in *Poets & Writers Magazine* (March/April 2011). Reprinted by permission of the publisher.

Alan Michael Parker. "Three Possibilities" from *The Ladder* (Tupelo). Copyright © 2016 by Alan Michael Parker. Reprinted by permission of Tupelo Press.

Chelsea Rathburn. "Still Life with Long-Range View." Copyright © 2016 by Chelsea Rathburn. First published in *The Cincinnati Review*. Reprinted by permission of the author.

Susan Rich. "*Boketto*." Copyright © 2017 by Susan Rich. First published in *Poem-a-Day*/Academy of American Poets. Reprinted by permission of the author.

Elizabeth Lindsey Rogers. "Abandoned Block Factory, Arkansas." Copyright © 2017 by Elizabeth Lindsey Rogers. First published in *Poem-a-Day*/Academy of American Poets. Reprinted by permission of the author.

Pattiann Rogers. "Geocentric" from *Geocentric* (Gibbs Smith). Copyright © 1993 by Pattiann Rogers. Reprinted by permission of the author.

Danielle Sellers. "Epithalamion for the Long Dead." Copyright © 2017 by Danielle Sellers. First published in *Prairie Schooner*. Reprinted by permission of the author.

Betsy Sholl. "Genealogy" from *Otherwise Unseeable*. Copyright © 2014 by the Board of Regents of the University of Wisconsin System. Reprinted courtesy of the University of Wisconsin Press.

Martha Silano. "Traveler's Lament" from *Blue Positive* (Steel Toe). Copyright © 2006 by Martha Silano. Reprinted by permission of the author.

Mark Smith-Soto. "Primrose Path." Copyright © 2016 by Mark Smith-Soto. First published in *Connotation Press*. Reprinted by permission of the author.

Wallace Stevens. "The Snow Man" from *The Collected Poems of Wallace Stevens*. Copyright © 1954 by Wallace Stevens and copyright renewed 1982 by Holly Stevens. Used by permission of Alfred A. Knopf, an imprint of the Knopf Doubleday Publishing Group, a division of Penguin Random House LLC. All rights reserved.

Maxine Susman. "Pulse." Copyright © 2017 by Maxine Susman. First published in *Journal of New Jersey Poets*. Reprinted by permission of the author.

Franz Wright. "Cloudless Snowfall" from *Walking to Martha's Vineyard*. Copyright © 2003 by Franz Wright. Used by permission of Alfred A. Knopf, an imprint of the Knopf Doubleday Publishing Group, a division of Penguin Random House LLC. All rights reserved.

Index

328

About the Editor

Diane Lockward is the editor of *The Crafty Poet II: A Portable Workshop* (Terrapin Books, 2016) and the earlier volume, *The Crafty Poet: A Portable Workshop* (Terrapin Books, rev. ed., 2016). She is also the author of four poetry books, most recently *The Uneaten Carrots of Atonement* (Wind Publications, 2016). Her awards include the Quentin R. Howard Poetry Prize, a poetry fellowship from the New Jersey State Council on the Arts, and a Woman of Achievement Award. Her poems have been included in such journals as *Harvard Review, Southern Poetry Review*, and *Prairie Schooner*. Her work has also been featured on *Poetry Daily, Verse Daily, The Writer's Almanac*, and Ted Kooser's *American Life in Poetry*. She is the founder, editor, and publisher of Terrapin Books.

CPSIA information can be obtained
at www.ICGtesting.com
Printed in the USA
LVHW010545180722
723709LV00007B/406

9 781947 896079